MW00511789

Praise For
Nine Lives of a Marriage
— a curious journey

"*'Nine Lives of a Marriage,' written by a Holocaust survivor, is one of the most important books of the day. This story is different from every other survivor story that has been written. Readers will be consumed by Eva and George's story of love and tears. So many women struggle today with the silence of infidelity. Eva's strength and persistence will serve as a role model for others. We will use this book in our congregation for book clubs and potentially even support groups.*"

Rabbi Peter S. Berg
Senior Rabbi, The Temple
Atlanta, GA

"*Most marriages are unlikely to survive long term infidelity, but when they do, it is because the couple is engaged in discussion, catharsis, negotiations, and ultimately resolution. Understanding how the Friedlanders resolve such complicated issues will no doubt provide valuable insights, not only to women, but to the therapists and clinicians working with individuals and couples facing similar challenges. This book fills a much needed niche in the literature on infidelity.*"

Linda Ligenza, ACSW
Bethesda, MD

"Women like Eva Friedlander, who are confronted with infidelity in a relationship, experience intense emotional pain, shame, loss of self-esteem — and for many who have already suffered trauma like the horrors of war, intense fear and a rekindling of mistrust. Mending a marriage takes work from both partners and learning how to rebuild individually and as a couple for a stronger bond. Goodman takes her readers on this journey as Eva and George declare a truce and rekindle their friendship at the end of his life."

Risa S. Fox, M.S., L.C.S.W.
Public Health Advisor
Center for Mental Health Services
SAMHSA, DHHS
Rockville, MD

"The story of Eva and George Friedlander is one that must be told. For forty years, the Friedlanders were our neighbors. We knew they were from Hungary, had been there during World War II, were Jews, and probably had experienced unimaginable wartime indignities. But we never asked questions.

It wasn't until later years that I learned from Eva what a remarkable story she had lived throughout most of her life. I'm an avid reader, but I've never come across a story like hers. Thank goodness she decided to put it to paper. Stunning as some of her revelations may be, it's all true and honestly told. It's a story that calls for print."

Mary Ann Lyon
Atlanta, GA

"In 'Nine Lives of a Marriage — A Curious Journey,' Mickey Goodman's portrayal of the Friedlanders' marriage gives a glimpse into the havoc and loss created by infidelity while showing how two Holocaust survivors survived one another's betrayal in a marriage of love and — ultimately — commitment. While both an interesting and beautiful story, the book would also serve as a guide and inspiration to women and men dealing with the hurt of infidelity in their own lives."

> Kelly Watton
> Travel Writer
> "Lonely Planet" and "Travelers' Tales"
> Roswell, GA

"Eva Friedlander's life story has all the ingredients for a best seller — survival though the horrors of the Holocaust and the other woman who invaded Eva's fifty-five-year marriage for forty-five of those tumultuous years. And that's just a hint of what to expect in this riveting beautifully written memoir."

> Adrienne Cohen
> Cohen Advertising
> Atlanta, GA

"After 40 plus years of friendship with George Friendlander, I can hardly wait to read the entire biography of such a great teacher and the only true intellect that I have met in my entire academic life. It will be quite an adventure to read about the man I thought I knew but maybe didn't."

Warren Weingrad
President of W&W Audio
Chemist
Atlanta, GA

Eva Friedlander (signature)

Nine Lives of a Marriage

– a curious journey

Eva Friedlander
with Mickey Goodman

Published by EDF Publishing
www.ninelivesofamarriage.com

Cover design by Heather Knorr
Editing by Judy Kirkwood, Reva Ezell, Karon Warren
Web design by http:// thesimplewebhost.com

Publishing support provided by Booklogix Publishing services, Alpharetta, Georgia

Manufactured in the United States of America

Library of Congress Cataloging-in-Publication Data
Eva Friedlander with Mickey Goodman.
Nine Lives of a Marriage — a curious journey: a memoir/Eva Friedlander

ISBN: 978-1-61005-008-1

1. Mickey Goodman, 2. Eva Friedlander, 3. Holocaust, 4. World War II, 5. Infidelity, 6. Budapest, 7. Hungary, 8. Italy, 9. Atlanta, 10. Jewish literature, 11. History

Bulk discounts are available to synagogues, groups, book clubs and fundraising campaigns.

For more information, contact Mickey Goodman:
Mickey@ninelivesofamarriage.com

A Note to the Reader

This book does not attempt to be all-encompassing. Rather, it is an account of my experiences during and after World War II and reveals some aspects of my life that may surprise many who know me.

Events, actions, experiences and their consequences over the years are recorded as I remember them. Some names have been changed, the time line has been compressed and the dialogue has been recreated from memory.

This is my story as I have lived it.

—Eva Friedlander

Eva Friedlander 1946

Foreword

For years friends and family have urged me to write my personal story bearing witness to the events of the Holocaust as it unfolded in Hungary. I hope it will ensure that my children and grandchildren will never forget the tragic events that led to the persecution and death of millions of Jews, including their cousins and grandfather.

This story spans three countries — Hungary, where I was born; Italy, my sojourn after the war; and America, the fulfillment of a life-long dream. It was here in America that my feelings of Jewish cultural identification were strengthened, here in a land where each person can affiliate with his or her religion without fear of reprisal.

The book traces my tempestuous marriage and anguish over my husband's infidelities. My personal reasons for staying in the marriage were many — love, loyalty, faith that things would improve and a shared history that only those who lived through the Holocaust can understand. But most significantly, I wanted to spare my children the trauma of a broken family such as I experienced in my childhood.

Infidelity, passion, betrayal, and forgiveness can happen anywhere and anytime. In the end, it is love that is important.

—*Eva Friedlander*

I was on assignment with the *Jewish Times* when I first met Eva and her husband, George, as he lay near death in a nursing home. He rallied to tell me his story — one of intrigue, deprivation, imprisonment and bravery during the Holocaust, as well as his accomplishments in Atlanta's thriving industrial chemical community.

It wasn't until months later when Eva asked if I would help her turn her story into a book that I learned of her personal anguish over his infidelity. I immediately felt that what Eva told me, coupled with George's experiences, would make a compelling book to add to the Holocaust literature and the annals of love. Both are tales of survival.

Eva and George overcame seemingly insurmountable obstacles in their lives, but it is her unshakable spirit and perseverance that makes her so remarkable. I hope readers will be as fascinated by the Friedlanders' story as I continue to be.

—*Mickey Goodman*

Acknowledgments

I want to thank my family, Dr. Lewis D. Friedlander, Dr. Lynne Friedlander, Judy Frieh, Marc Goldman, Eva Marie and Katarina Friedlander and Jeremy and Ella Goldman for their love and support. Thanks also to friends who encouraged me to tell my story, to Barbara Blackford, Cheri Eisenberg and Roger Elam for their help, and to Survivors of the Shoah Visual History Foundation and The William Breman Jewish Heritage and Holocaust Museum for inviting me to record my experiences of the Holocaust. I would also like to thank Mickey Goodman for helping bring my story to life.

— *Eva Friedlander*

Love and thanks to my children and grandchildren who bring me great joy every day — David, Nathan, Beth, Jamise, Sonny, Megan, Jenna, Mia, Jael and Idan. Also to my talented writer friends who encouraged me through the process — Fran Kaplan, Echo Garrett, Margie Goldsmith, Irene Levine, Hilary Nangle — to our book editor Judy Kirkwood, and graphic designer, Heather Knorr. To my BFF, Judy Giles — thanks for taking me to the Margaret Mitchell House all those years ago to give me the inspiration and courage to begin a writing career when I felt I was long past my prime.

—*Mickey Goodman*

PROLOGUE

ATLANTA, GEORGIA — 2004

NurseCare of Buckhead

The moment the door opened and *she* stepped in, tension ricocheted around the nursing home room faster than bullets from a German Luger.

George apparently felt it too.

"Eva? What is it? Are you still here?" he asked.

"I'm here," I replied, trying not to reveal my inner turmoil. "So is your other regular visitor." I stared at the door, taken aback by the woman standing before me.

In my mind's eye, she was still that voluptuous bombshell who had looked at him adoringly long ago and purred, "Oh, George. You say the most fascinating things." But the woman who had once oozed sexuality and commanded attention in a crowded room had lost her appeal. Oh, I could see remnants of the old Sadie. Her hair was newly coiffed and her makeup was perfection. She was standing too far away, but I assumed her nails were freshly painted. Today, she wouldn't catch a passing glance from a man on the prowl — much less George, who had a discerning eye. Did he imagine her as a young woman? Or the way she looked the last time he actually saw her before the fall that blinded him?

For once, the brilliant man who had charmed countless women with his flattery, talked his way out of three Hungarian forced labor camps, a man who spoke six languages — was speechless.

"I'm so, so sorry. So sorry," she stammered. "I must be early, I'll come back later."

George turned his head in the direction of our voices and his face lit up. He flashed that famous grin that had charmed women throughout his eighty-one years. "Stay," he said. "Both of you. Please."

I felt a combination of amazement and fury. After all the decades of acrimony, how could George ask me to share his hospital room with Sadie, the woman who had been the third person in my marriage for forty-five years?

~~~~

Out of 825,000 Jews living in Hungary prior to the outbreak of World War II, approximately 550,000 were murdered during the Holocaust, including most of those in forced labor camps. Throughout Europe, the Judenrein (eradication of the Jews) evolved slowly over time. In Hungary, it took just 54 days.

—The Jewish Virtual Library, A Division of the American-Israeli Cooperative Enterprise

PART I

BUDAPEST, HUNGARY – 1945

Chapter 1

In 1945, Budapest was in chaos and so were our lives. While some streets were largely intact, others had been obliterated by the relentless bombings. Belongings were missing, likely confiscated by the Nazis, and even essential documents like birth certificates, marriage licenses and property deeds had been scattered by the winds of war. For many, it was hard to know where to begin picking up the pieces.

That's where I came in. Finally, after more than two years in hiding from both the Hungarian Arrow Cross who hated Jews and the Nazis bent on exterminating us all, I took charge of my own life and established my own business, something few women in the 1940s attempted.

My secretarial services, designed to help people track down important papers, send correspondence, and translate documents, met with instant success and I discovered that while I was infinitely capable of navigating the tangle of bureaucracy, I couldn't seem to manage my own heart. All it took was the "vroom, vroom" of an engine and the emergence of the handsome chemist turned diplomat who would become my husband to send me reeling.

But then who could resist George Friedlander? Everyone in my little secretarial shop stood with mouths agape. Even Mother's steady click-clicking on the typewriter came to a halt as all eyes turned toward the longest, sleekest Italian Aero two-seater convertible we had ever seen. It seemed downright decadent in a city where so many citizens still lacked basic shelter and food.

I couldn't decide which was more dazzling, the silver sports car with its butternut leather interior or the handsome young driver who emerged. He was trim with a crown of dark wavy hair and arresting blue eyes. I ogled him outrageously, my gaze slowly drifting from his face to his broad shoulders draped in a heavy khaki American military-style trench coat with the collar rakishly turned up. It was so luxurious; I had to put my hand in my skirt pocket to keep from stroking the heavy fabric.

A few moments passed before I noticed the exotic looking young woman with erect posture and smug attitude who emerged behind him. She was wearing an identical trench coat, right down to the turned-up collar. In a clear effort to establish ownership, she tucked her hand through the crook of his arm possessively as he turned his attention to me.

"My name is *Dr.* George Friedlander," he said, smiling and reaching out his hand to shake mine. "I'm the new Italian ambassador to Hungary and I need help setting up an office to repatriate displaced Italian soldiers and expedite their safe return home. I believe my father, Louis Friedlander, told you to expect me." Almost as an afterthought, he turned toward the haughty young woman sending daggers my way. "This is Luba, my assistant," he said.

Luba turned on her heel, sat on top of one of the empty desks and pouted as George locked his blue eyes onto mine. "I also need to hire a staff quickly," he smiled disarmingly. "Can you get started tomorrow?"

He pulled a lengthy list from his pocket and handed it to me. "We'll need furniture and basic office equipment like you have here — only more of it," he said, glancing around. "My father thinks highly of your secretarial and translation services. I'm sure I will too."

He motioned to Luba and they abruptly turned to leave. It wasn't until they roared off in the Aero that I realized I had never agreed to work with him.

Skepticism was written all over Mother's face. "He's just like Andras and the other slick young men who hang all over you only he's richer," she complained. "I'll be surprised if we ever see him again."

The shop returned to normal and Mother to her typing. A few more customers stepped through the door, happy to have found a small business that could help them reclaim their lives. Generally, our clients dropped things off on their way to work and returned at the end of the day to retrieve them; but for those who chose to wait, we served a cup of steaming ersatz espresso. You might say we were a 1940s version of Starbucks and Kinko's.

Mother grumbled all that afternoon, a clear sign that it was not going to be a pleasant evening. To coax her out of her funk, I calculated our profits for the day and bribed her with a take-out dinner from a neighborhood diner where the savory blends of meat and fresh vegetables set our stomachs growling. After months of near starvation, everything tasted wonderful, particularly her favorite Blue Plate special, liver and onions with mashed potatoes.

I volunteered to pick dinner up while mother remained at the shop, hoping to snag a few additional customers. It posed no hardship on either of us. She preferred to stay and finish up work and I wanted a few minutes alone to relive George's dramatic entry.

When George's father had come to tell me that George would be stopping by, even he admitted his son was an enigma. "George earned a doctorate in chemistry from the University of Bologna, yet he is returning to Budapest as a diplomat," he told us. "It doesn't make sense even to me, but I suppose he used his considerable charm to talk them into giving him the position."

I couldn't come to grips about my fascination for this man, but I couldn't deny I hoped against hope that he would return, as promised.

Much to Mother's amazement, George not only returned, he brought a huge box of official documents for translation. Mother was downright civil — until he told her he had come to pick me up to search for an office. Her frown said volumes.

"I can't leave my mother alone with all the work," I sputtered, looking from his smiling face to her furrowed brow.

George ignored her body language, set the box on her desk, and then patiently explained what needed to be done. By the time he had finished, she was bobbing her head in assent and even wore a faint smile. Without further ado, he took me by the elbow, steered me out the door, and began asking about my taste in movies, food, and music.

Despite the heavy volume of additional business George brought in, Mother rarely missed an opportunity to bring up my engagement to Dan Gonda, who was still in a Ukrainian work camp after more than three years. "Have you heard from your fiancé, Dan recently?" she'd ask pointedly. George grinned at her obvious tactics, but continued to woo me with abandon, plying me with chocolates — a rare delicacy — and taking me out for sandwiches and dessert at Gerbeaud on Vörösmarty Square where the Dobos Tortes, seven layer cakes with caramel sugar topping that glowed like topaz, were irresistible.

Many days I was lost in a daze. Somehow, I managed to run the shop, bring in new customers, and work with another important diplomat, British attaché Robert Graham, who spoke Hungarian fluently, not an easy task for those schooled in Romance languages. Through him, I met many influential Americans, Russians, Hungarians, and Brits, who proved to be a great help to me in the future.

George and I quickly located a suitable building for his office not far from my little shop and began purchasing furniture. Since new merchandise was scarce, we perused various open-air markets for much more upscale office furniture and equipment than Mother and I had been able to afford. The office took shape quickly and George opened the doors for business.

If Luba did a lick of work, I was never aware of it. Ever present in George's office, she was like a bee buzzing annoyingly overhead who never returned to her hive — wherever that was.

George's primary assignment was to account for perhaps hundreds of Italian soldiers who had been left behind in the chaos of the Axis retreat and to retrieve abandoned military vehicles. Most of the soldiers remained in hiding, fearing both Hungarians who despised anyone who sided with the Germans and the often vicious liberating Russian army. Who could blame them? Their fear left them in a Catch 22 position: terrified to emerge, but unable to return home without travel documents, identification papers, and transportation — all items George could expedite. To get the word out, we posted public notices and purchased newspaper ads. We also relied on word of mouth. As soon as a few Italian soldiers met with success, others trickled in.

As the weeks flew by, my growing feelings for George consumed me. I thought about him every minute we weren't together and dreamed of sleeping in his arms. Luba apparently saw the handwriting on the wall and simply disappeared. When I asked George about her, he shrugged. "She used me as a way to get out of Italy," he said. "Besides, she was a terrible typist."

I knew George minimized what was surely a sexual relationship, but I breathed a sigh of relief that she was no longer a romantic threat. In retrospect, I should have wondered why he cast her off like a pair of dirty socks as soon as he met me.

Discounting Dan, who was out of sight, out of mind, George obviously thought he was the only man in my life. When he came into the shop unexpectedly one day, he found me preparing to leave with one of our customers, Andras, a wickedly handsome married man who flirted outrageously with me. I had never encouraged a romantic relationship, but was always grateful when he roared up to the curb in the cast-off German motorcycle he had found on the side of the road and invited me to the country to buy fresh food. We always came home loaded with delectables like smoked meat, creamy hand-churned butter, eggs, fruits, vegetables, and freshly baked bread — items either unavailable or unaffordable on the black market.

Still, there was no mistaking that George had stolen my heart and I wasn't the only one. His return to Budapest was marked by an interview in a magazine called *"The Theater."*

"The role of a diplomat is like a physician," he told the reporter. "People are still hurting and bleeding and they need first aid." His comments sent my heart thumping and reflected a softer side I hadn't seen. It made me love him all the more. In what I came to know as "vintage George," he appeared to be an expert in a thousand areas, including politics. He explained that the new Italian government was doing "an energetic job to eradicate the old regime" and getting considerable help from Pope Pius XII.

The celebrity status of being interviewed in the paper even impressed my mother. I caught her showing the article to friends. "This is our new, best customer, George Friedlander," she told them. "On the opposite side of the page is an article about Robert Graham, the British attaché Eva works with." What a strange coincidence that interviews about my two most important clients and favorite men were not only in the same newspaper but side by side on the same page.

As the days passed, George stopped by our shop on the flimsiest excuse. One day he asked, "Do you have a bathing suit on under your dress? Girls I date should be ready to go swimming at a moment's notice."

It wasn't an idle comment. He began swooping me up for a mid-day swim in the Olympic-size indoor-outdoor pool on Margaret Island, the famous resort and park situated in the center of the Danube. Known for its healing waters, the resort had somehow survived the Allied bombings and was accessible by the Margaret Bridge, one of the few to be spared. Unlike most resorts that restricted use of the facilities to guests, Margaret Island welcomed Hungarian residents and tourists alike to swim in the famous pools and dine in their restaurants.

George was such a fascinating, handsome, entertaining, and intelligent man, with an offbeat sense of humor, it was easy to fall for him. I suppose he initially attracted to me because of my looks, but as time wore on, he told me how much he admired my entrepreneurial and managerial skills.

At the same time, I was filled with guilt. Until George entered the picture, I had indulged in only minor flirtations, making it clear to everyone that I was waiting for Dan's return. Like a circus performer, I teetered precariously on a tightrope, wanting to grab the trapeze and fly, while at the same time experiencing a fear of heights. Soon, I suspected, Dan would be released and I would have to make an agonizing decision.

Mother was no help. She constantly pointed out the differences between Dan's family and the Friedlanders: Dan's was so accepting, George's so aloof. "Your grandparents pointed out your father's faults, but I refused to see them until it was too late," she warned. "He was handsome and charming, just like George. And George will someday break your heart just as your father broke mine."

Chapter 2

During the weeks that followed, George introduced me to the few surviving members of his old crowd. They seldom spoke of the many friends who perished during their internments in forced labor camps, or places like Auschwitz. They reminisced, instead, about the carefree times when soccer, girls, jazz, and schoolwork were at the forefront and the future seemed limitless.

"I was a pretty cocky teenager and disagreed with my father on most topics," George confessed. "After one particularly bad row over a foolish purchase, I packed my suitcase and announced loudly that I was leaving to make my fortune. I was determined to show my father that it was easy to make money."

Fortuitously, the father of a friend owned a hotel in Budapest and was in need of an assistant manager. He not only hired George, he allowed him to live on-site in one of the staff rooms. "I made myself useful wherever I could and because I could speak Hungarian, English, French, German, Italian, and a passable Russian, the owner came to rely on me whenever we had foreign guests."

A Greek delegation posed a particularly thorny problem. They had traveled to Budapest because they heard that Hungarian horses were among the fastest in the world and wanted introductions to breeders.

"You've come to the right man," George told them. "I've had vast experience with horses and would be happy to assist you with the transaction." In actuality, he was a city boy and knew nothing about race horses, but his Uncle Artur, the black sheep of the family, was well versed on the subject. "My father disowned him because he gambled his share of his family's fortune on a thoroughbred who never won a race. If he got wind that I had formed a partnership with Uncle Artur, I knew my father would disown me too. For me, it was a partnership made in heaven and a quick way to make a bundle."

As usual, George's well-honed instincts were right on target and Uncle Artur introduced him to a gypsy who purchased horses from breeders. Both were eager to assist George for a cut of the profits and after a few minutes of negotiations, they struck a deal to split the proceeds.

The odd bedfellows toured the countryside for a few days to scout out the best horses and make contacts with villagers. At night, they dined with the Greeks to report their findings. "A few days later, I drove out to the country in a rented limousine with the Greeks, the gypsy, and Uncle Artur," George said. "It was a great trip. The Greeks bought two horses and in short order all of us made sizeable profits."

George was so anxious to show off to his father that he walked into a fancy dealership and bought the most expensive car on the showroom floor, an electric blue Alfa Romeo.

That first evening after his return home, his father looked out their balcony window and spied the Alfa Romeo parked under the street lamp. "Who do you suppose owns that expensive vehicle?" he asked George, his voice filled with envy.

George's moment of triumph had arrived. "Why, that's mine," he told him nonchalantly. "I bought it with the earnings from my job. Would you like to take a spin?"

Mr. Friedlander's reaction was not what George expected. "What were you thinking?" he yelled. "You should have put all that money in the bank for your education instead of throwing it away on a fancy car."

George's teenage escapades were the polar opposite of mine. I had never set foot outside of Hungary. George had not only traveled extensively with his family, he was one of three students sent to Rome as a reward for writing the best essay on Roman antiquities. "My love affair with that ancient city began the moment I set foot on Italian soil," he said. "I was surrounded by all the places I had read and written about. Seeing them in person was the best education I received. Up until then, I had vacillated about where to attend college, but the first thing I said to my father when I got back home was, "'I want to study chemistry in Italy.'"

My teenage years were so different. While George and his friends studied for high school exams, I had to drop out before graduation to attend secretarial school and help support my mother. George played soccer, flirted with girls, saw movies and listened to American jazz in smoke-filled cafés while I worked in a stuffy law office with adults twice my age. Except for my childhood friend, Edit, I had very little social life.

I lived vicariously through George and his friends, particularly George (Zsuti) Guttman, a lifetime comrade. The two Georges found humor in everything and were a constant source of entertainment for all around them. If one started a sentence, the other would finish it, then both would burst out laughing, drawing everyone into their circle. They also had an intellectual connection I both admired and envied.

When Zsuti began writing and translating American musicals, George would often supply the perfect word to fit the storyline and poetic meter. Zsuti's Hungarian translations of musicals, ranging from "West Side Story" and "Hello Dolly" to "The Fantastics" and "Can Can," won many awards and as his celebrity mounted, his nickname brought instant recognition. So great was his fame that after his death in 1995 — a devastating blow to George — the Hungarian government affixed a bronze plaque to his house. It was a testament to the Hungarians' admiration for their country's most celebrated poet and lyricist.

I also never tired of hearing tales about the opulent Café New York, a famous restaurant frequented by the crème de la crème of society and an eclectic crowd of theater-goers, actors, artists, writers, and poets. The ornate establishment was built in 1894 and had magnificent gilded moldings, Oriental carpets, incredible hand-painted murals, and Venetian glass chandeliers. In fact, the décor was so regal that people compared it to the Hapsburg Palace in Vienna.

Because it was located in the heart of the theater district, critics stopped by on opening night to pen their midnight reviews over a glass of brandy. A number of patrons came just for the fine food and rare wines, but the majority came to rub elbows with colorful patrons like the glamorous Gabor sisters, Zsa Zsa, Eva, and Magda. The boys admitted to flirting openly with the sisters, who returned the favor three-fold. George, who seemed to take pride in revealing his previous conquests, hinted broadly that he had a tryst with one of the sisters, but was uncharacteristically coy about naming her.

Both before and after the war, George moved seamlessly from academic circles to theatrical crowds and befriended a number of struggling artists and actors who lived in modest, crowded apartments near the Café, their home away from home. The motley group regularly spent entire evenings bantering about theater, art, politics, and literature while nursing a single bowl of hearty soup or a glass of cheap wine.

"Instead of kicking out the Bohemian crowd who attracted well-heeled customers, management catered to them, fully aware that this eclectic group of artists was among the main attractions," George said. "The waiters were ordered not to harass them, no matter how long they lingered. One night when I joined them, we sat at a window table for so long that I fell asleep. A waiter gave me a gentle nudge. 'Sir,' he told me. 'Sleeping patrons are not a good advertisement for our establishment.'"

Sadly, the Café New York remained closed even after the liberation, so I didn't get to see it until many, many years later when I returned to Budapest to see my mother. He made it up to me by taking me to other fine restaurants opening throughout the city and inviting me to his home for dinner. The first time I went to the Friedlanders, I was a nervous wreck and went to great pains to iron my best dress and polish my shoes until they shone. I even splurged and had a pair of nylons rewoven. Though costly, the repair was far cheaper than trying to buy a new pair on the black market.

What a miserable evening it was. Though the delicious meal was served on a table set with fine linen, china, and crystal, Mrs. Friedlander went out of her way to make me feel uncomfortable that evening and all those that followed. She made no bones that I was clearly unworthy of her son's affections and held herself so erect I thought she might fall over backwards. Never once did she use the familial "te" (you) when referring to me, preferring the more formal "maga" as if I were a total stranger.

If I complimented her on particularly lovely porcelain or a fine painting, she was quick to point out that the item had come from the most expensive store in Budapest before the war. If I mentioned a book I had read recently, she indicated that intellectual pursuits were far less important to her than material objects. She even bragged to me about the daughter of a rich friend who had returned after studying in Switzerland, making it crystal clear that she preferred a rich, socially connected wife for George rather than a mere legal secretary.

Mr. Friedlander was not much better. Only Klari, George's sweet sister, was welcoming. She thanked me for helping her brother establish his office and always had a nice word to say about how I looked or the work I was doing. She seemed clearly embarrassed by the snooty attitude of her parents and made sure to point out the obvious flaws in their fine home, like the hundreds of bullet holes in the stone work outside, souvenirs from the Allied bombings.

Much as I hated to admit it, I could understand his parents' point of view. Our families had little in common. The Friedlanders had come through the war virtually unscathed and were accustomed to indulging their children with the best clothing, education, and cultural opportunities. Because Jews were not allowed to attend university in Hungary, George's father had sent him to Italy to study chemistry, as he wanted, and planned to send Klari to one of the fine finishing schools in London. It was clear that in their eyes I would never be a social equal.

Their blatant disapproval didn't faze George or our budding relationship. He seemed intent on winning my love, and I was mesmerized by this Renaissance man. He had a Ph.D. in chemistry and could have serious conversations with scholars, but felt equally at home arguing with professional musicians about who was the best among American jazz performers — Ella Fitzgerald, Louis Armstrong, Dizzie Gillespie, or Duke Ellington. Though he never had a formal lesson, George could sit down at a piano bar and play any tune requested by patrons or pick up a paintbrush and canvas and reproduce a lovely Monet. If he learned a new language, he was not content until he had studied the history, art, and architecture of the country.

There was no one else like George.

Chapter 3

Although we spent many evenings with George's friends and their girlfriends, we often stole time to drive across the Danube to Buda and linger over cappuccino and pogácsa (scones) at the historic Café Ruszwurm, on Castle Hill near the Royal Palace. I loved hearing about his university years in Italy, a country whose art and architecture I had studied and longed to see. His descriptions were so vivid I could almost smell garlicky tomato sauce wafting through cafes and picture the beautiful, carefree young people who strolled along the historic streets of Bologna and Rome.

He was so taken by their classical features that he snapped dozens of pictures of his landlady's lovely daughter, Lucilla. One photo he took of her standing barefoot in the garden as she pruned shrubs was extremely striking and he proudly showed it to a friend. Weeks later, the friend called to tell him excitedly that his photo had wound up in a popular local magazine. "I supposed that the camera store sold it without my permission and although I was flattered that the publication thought it worth printing, I would have been happier if they had paid me for it or at least credited me with taking it," he complained.

One of the proudest days of his life came in 1941 when he graduated from the University of Bologna with a doctorate in chemistry. "When I turned the diploma over and read the back, I was furious. It identified me as a member of the 'Jewish race.' What a slap in the face. Was not a Jew worthy of this high honor without a disclaimer?"

Following graduation, George remained in Italy for a few months, but longed to be back in Hungary with his family and friends. In the interim, he somehow became connected with the Underground. In his file cabinet, I found several letters of introduction from the secret Zionist organization in Budapest urging other representatives to "help him in all cases where necessity should arise and expedite his case."

"I taught some of them how to blow up German trains," he told me proudly. "We put slow reacting chemicals on sponges and threw them into the coal cars while they were being loaded, then ran like fury. Within minutes, the chemicals reacted with coal dust and exploded. We knocked out a couple of locomotives, some box cars loaded with ammunition and a troop transport train."

Another assignment involved helping transport Jewish refugees to the coast of Italy. "We secured false train routings to disguise the mission, got fake papers for the refugees, and dressed them like injured German soldiers. I rode up front with the engineer and laughed every time we got the train through another checkpoint without mishap. We smuggled nearly one-hundred Jews to the Italian border where they were picked up by members of the Haganah and Irgun and spirited into Israel under the noses of the British." His passionate support of the Zionist movement continued long after we arrived in America.

In addition to his exploits with the Underground, George boasted about his many international affairs. Since I had seen him work his considerable charm on women, I was not put off. Instead, I was foolishly flattered that he had chosen me over the illustrious assortment of beauties that fawned at his feet. It should have been an indication of things to come.

Over time, George told me about his ordeal during the war. "With the clouds of war looming overhead in 1942, I should have known better than to come home," he said, "but I missed my family. It was a huge mistake. Two weeks after I arrived, the Germans invaded."

The rest is history. By May, the Nazis had pressured leaders of the Hungarian Arrow Cross party who were tucked snuggly into their pockets to begin rounding up young Jewish men to perform manual labor for the army. At first, George avoided the roundup by doing public service in a hospital. But as pressure increased on Jewish leaders to supply more and more men, he, too, was ordered to report.

"We were told to bring our own food, clothing, blankets, and canteens. My mother sewed gold coins under the lining of my belt and reminded me over and over to sleep in my fine new leather boots so they wouldn't be stolen," he said. His last sight of his parents was of them standing on the steps of their apartment building weeping.

At the train station where he reported, George recognized many friends, all hoping to be assigned together. It was not to be. Many were loaded on boxcars and sent to the Ukraine near the Russian border where the weather was as much an enemy as the Russian guards. Others were bound for Austria near the German border. George was a bit luckier. He was assigned to Kôszeg, a labor camp between Budapest and Vienna. "There was no fence, but the perimeter was patrolled by guards and vicious dogs trained to kill on command. They were more terrifying than the guards."

Shortly after his arrival, George and other prisoners were forced to witness the punishment for an attempted escape. "The guards didn't fire a shot, but the carnage was unspeakable," he said. "They shoved the two escapees into cages and ordered the dogs to attack the poor bastards. Mercifully, one prisoner was bitten on the jugular and died quickly. The second wasn't as fortunate. His bloodcurdling screams and the ferocious barking of the dogs still ring in my ears. The more blood the dogs tasted, the more vicious they became. The guards stood by gloating and laughing, egging the dogs on as the poor prisoner begged them to shoot him. Finally, I guess the sadists became bored with their 'sport' and fired a single shot through his temple."

This incident and others involving dogs trained to kill precipitated recurring nightmares that haunted the remainder of George's life. Even as he lay in the nursing home decades later, he would wake up in a cold sweat and describe being pursued by barking dogs. He always felt he was just one step ahead of death.

Life in camp was brutal. Prisoners slept on wooden slat bunk beds without mattresses and those who hadn't brought their own blankets nearly froze in the unheated barracks. Everyone slept in a coat and used their extra clothing for pillows. Though the guards complained constantly about "the stinking Jews," there was no opportunity to bathe or wash clothing. In desperation, many plunged into the frigid river when they could, regardless of the weather, but even those opportunities were few and far between. To further erode the morale of prisoners, letters from home were often delayed for weeks or tossed away.

Days ran into weeks and weeks into months, but the routine never varied. Each morning they were awakened at daybreak, served a breakfast of watery soup and moldy bread and marched out to the fields at bayonet point. Some prisoners dug trenches, others hauled rocks or worked on the roads; the worst job was digging mass graves. The work was brutal and if prisoners sat down to rest they were beaten or shot. By evening, the malnourished prisoners were marched back to their barracks where they dropped into an exhausted sleep.

"In the beginning, they allowed our families to visit for a brief few hours once a month and my parents made every effort to come and bring clean clothing and food that would keep without refrigeration," George said. "They were my life line."

Another bright spot at Kôszeg was sharing a bunk bed with his Bohemian friend, Alfonso, a Vaudeville-type actor and comedian who taught him card and magic tricks that saved his life more than once. A quick learner, George became as adept as Alfonso and it wasn't long before the two hatched a plan to elicit favors from two young guards assigned to their barracks.

"Each night we'd do card and magic tricks and tell jokes especially for them," George said. "They loved it, especially when the jokes were at the expense of Alfonso who had only one pair of socks and no opportunity to wash them or even air them out. You could smell his feet from a mile away. They also guffawed at our stories about Father Holma, a randy fictitious priest. The more they drank, the more they appreciated our attempts at humor."

After a particularly raucous evening when the guards were liberally imbibing, George half-jokingly asked for weekend passes. To his surprise, the guards agreed. Several weekends later, George and Alphonso clutched the passes in their hands and thumbed a ride to Budapest, never intending to return to Kôszeg.

Their freedom was short-lived. George was picked up a few weeks later and sent to a second forced labor camp near the Ukraine border where security was far more stringent and the weather frigid. Because of their desertion, Alfonso was sent elsewhere and the friends were never able to reconnect.

At the second labor camp, the guards were even more brutal than those at Kôszeg. At one point, George was beaten so severely without provocation that he lost several teeth and developed an infection which went untreated. He lived under constant fear of death, either through severe beatings or starvation.

The one bright light was an intelligent young architectural student named Miklos who George befriended. "I've heard that German and Hungarian doctors are doing experiments on mental patients," he told George. "They're always on the lookout for subjects. If we could figure a way to fake instability, maybe the experiments would be easier than pounding rocks to smithereens. At least we'd be inside."

George's imagination took flight. "I knew enough about schizophrenia to mimic the symptoms," he told me, "and I knew I could teach Miklos too." During the day while they were out in the field digging trenches, they formulated a plan. Night after night, they turned their erratic behavior up a notch and deliberately awakened the other prisoners with their blood curdling screams. The guards came running. "We knew that if our plan backfired, we could get shot, but neither of us had much hope of coming out alive."

The plan worked like a charm and it wasn't long before they were labeled "schizoid" and hauled off to the medical barracks. Unlike their old barracks where no one cared whether they slept in their clothing, the nurse demanded their boots. But George and Miklos kicked and screamed so loudly she must have decided it would be easier to just leave them alone. The duo knew if they ever had a chance to escape in the snow, they had to have their boots.

"The first morning, the guards came to get us before we had even eaten and marched us into the hospital barracks," he said. "A doctor strapped my arms, legs, and torso to a gurney, then connected my head to some kind of electrical machine. When he put a wad of paper in my mouth, I panicked, particularly when one of the aides explained to another that it was so 'the poor crazy bastard won't bite his tongue off.' The last thing I remember before losing consciousness was the horrible rattle of the machine and a pain more intense than anything I had ever experienced."

When George woke up hours later, he could barely raise his head to look around and every bone in his body ached. Out of the corner of his eye he saw Miklos lying frighteningly still. The beds on either side were vacant, a stark reminder that prisoners used in medical experiments were expendable.

"My mind was as fragmented as a jigsaw puzzle," he said. "I couldn't make the pieces fit together. Had they killed Miklos?" When his friend finally roused and the two were able to talk, George surmised they had been guinea pigs in a new mental health treatment called electroshock therapy that he had heard discussed in scientific circles while he was studying in Italy.

"If that's what they're doing, then it's likely they're trying to determine therapeutic versus lethal doses," I told him. "We're lucky to be alive, but those barbarians who call themselves scientists might kill us the next time. We've got to get out of here."

Despite their still foggy minds and aching bodies, they managed to throw tantrums again that night. "I guess we pushed one nurse over the edge because she told us if we didn't shut up, she'd send us to Auschwitz," George said. "I thought I knew European geography, but I had never heard of such a place."

After she left, Miklos whispered, "Auschwitz is a camp where the Germans gas Jews to death," he said. The grim thought sent vibrations racing up George's spine and he made up his mind that he was willing to take his chances with the very real threat of the dogs rather than to submit to more shock treatments — or worse.

The following night brought the perfect opportunity. The clouds drooped down like low hanging fruit, a sign that fog would descend and provide cover — at least for a while. As soon as the new patients settled down, George and Miklos crept out in their stocking feet to avoid making a sound, carrying their precious boots. Creeping toward the warehouses where "normal" prisoners slept, George pulled on his boots, waited for the guards and dogs to make their rounds at the far end of the camp and made a run for the surrounding woods that sloped down toward a narrow stream. "The fog was thicker than my mother's potato soup and provided the perfect cover," George said. "I virtually disappeared. I've never run so fast before or since and I assumed Miklos was right behind me."

Throughout the night, George trilled the secret whistle he and his friend had practiced. As the hours passed, he grew hoarse and also afraid the guards would follow the sound of a strange bird call in such a dense fog. Finally, he heard Miklos's answering trill and his knees buckled with relief. "We hugged one another and wept like long lost brothers," he said.

Their joyful reunion was mitigated by the precariousness of their situation. If they wanted to put some distance between themselves and the camp, time was of the essence. "We walked toward the middle of the frozen riverbed so the dogs would have trouble following our scent," George said. "Every now and then, we fell through thin ice and the bitter cold water seeped through our boots, turning our toes into painful cubes of ice."

Near total exhaustion and in danger of hypothermia and frostbite, they spotted a farm in the distance and debated whether they should take their chances and hide in the barn or keep walking and freeze to death. They chose the relative warmth of the barn, which fortunately was void of livestock, giving the farmer little reason to investigate.

George and Miklos remained under a blanket of hay in the loft for two days, sleeping and waking day and night, too afraid to emerge, even for food or water. On the third morning, they struck out for a tiny village they had spotted from the loft window.

"It was surreal," said George. "The peasant woman who sold us the bread and milk didn't even ask who we were, where we were from, or why I paid her with a gold coin instead of *forints*. She was probably so dazzled by the sight of real gold that she decided to pocket the money and report us later."

Once the purchases were made, they half-ran, half-stumbled back to the barn, devoured two loaves of bread and washed it down with the fresh milk. "We ate it so ravenously, we barely tasted it," George said.

After their brazen forage, they didn't budge for another two nights until their empty stomachs forced them out again. Instead of returning to the village where they were afraid the peasant woman had reported them to the Nazis, they decided to raid the farmer's kitchen. As soon as they heard the family leave, they stole into the house.

Not only was there bread on the counter, a slab of smoked pork hung on a hook from the ceiling.

"It was the first meat we had seen since leaving Budapest," George said. "I knew my rabbi would rather starve than eat bacon but at that point I didn't care. Miklos grabbed the bread, I pulled down the pork, and we left as silently as we had entered. Once out the door, I whispered, 'What would our dear Father Holma think of our stealing this poor farmer's food?'"

Miklos retorted, "I think he would say, 'Grab a flask of wine on the way out!'" Subduing laughter, they stopped by the well to quench their thirst, hoping that a small amount of water remained in the bottom of the bucket. Though it was barely enough to satisfy their thirst, they knew that cranking the handle to lower the bucket was out of the question. The squeaking would set off an avalanche of problems.

Hungry and frightened of discovery, they slunk back into the barn and crept up to their snug hiding place in the loft, but as soon as their stomachs were full, fear set in. What if the farmer came searching for the thieves who had helped themselves to his food?

"We argued back and forth about whether to stay or leave and finally decided to wend our way toward Budapest. In retrospect, it was not our best idea," George said. "As we were crossing the road to return to the riverbed, a Hungarian army truck flew around the corner. We knew if we ran, the soldiers would shoot us. If we raised our hands in surrender, chances were good they would kill us anyway."

Almost in unison, they raised their hands. The soldiers made a joke about two more stupid Jews trying to escape and shoved them into the back of a truck alongside other exhausted escapees. Most, including George and Miklos, were dozing off when the truck came to an abrupt halt deep in the countryside. Off in the distance, they could make out another camp and everyone immediately feared that like other prisoners they had heard about, they would be forced to dig a mass grave, then line up on the edge to be shot. George wondered who among the prisoners the guards would select to shovel dirt on their former colleagues before they, too, were killed. With each step farther from the truck, fear mounted.

"The sight was hard to comprehend," George rasped. "When the full impact hit me, I vomited. Dangling grotesquely from tree branches were fifty to sixty frozen naked bodies. One of the soldiers picked up his gun and took pot shots as if he were at target practice."

George paused, blinking back tears. I took his hand in mine. "You don't have to go on," I told him. "You never have to tell me if it's too painful."

He brushed away the tears, then continued with the gruesome story. "One by one, the other soldiers raised their guns and fired, laughing at their new game. I considered making a run for it, but there was some reason they didn't just get on with their sport and kill us too. Were their orders to bring us back to Budapest? After what seemed like an eternity, they yelled obscenities and warned us about experiencing the same fate if we dared attempt another escape.

"We spoke not another word the rest of the way. I couldn't get the sight out of my mind. How had this atrocity happened? Had the prisoners just lined up like lambs for the slaughter? I vowed that even though my decision not to run had been wise this time, I would never again just wait to be shot."

Within hours after their arrival at the deportation center, George found himself on a train headed toward the very camp Miklos had talked about with such fear — the one rumored to be a gateway to Auschwitz. If he had any chance of survival, he would have to find a way to escape before it was too late.

"I bided my time, looking for a weak link in the system," he said. "A window of opportunity opened when I befriended a teenage guard who was achingly homesick for his family and girlfriend. Each night, I entertained him with my card and magic tricks and dumb jokes about Father Holma," George said. "Before long, he confided that he was trying to save money to marry his girlfriend 'after the Axis victory.' I had found my opportunity to put the gold coins to good use."

George put on the performance of his life and ended with making a gold coin disappear behind the young guard's ear. After it miraculously re-appeared, he casually dropped the coin at his feet. The guard's eyes lit up with envy.

"The kid asked me to do it again so he could figure out how I did it," George said. "I repeated the trick, letting him get a close look at the coin so he could calculate what it might purchase — likely enough for a proper engagement ring."

Then George offered him a deal: the coin for a complete Hungarian officer's uniform and military ID. "If I had misjudged the boy, he would report me to his superiors. On the other hand, if I had read him right, I could escape before being shipped to Auschwitz."

It went precisely as planned. The young guard received the coveted coin and George got the uniform. Since officers could come and go at will from the camp, no one even asked for his identification papers and he hitched a ride aboard a military truck bound for Budapest, praying he would find his family still alive.

His return just days before Hungary's liberation was fraught with danger. Allied bombs were indiscriminate; while some streets were unscathed, others were completely obliterated. Though the Friedlander family home was intact, another family was in residence and he dared not try to reclaim it. Impersonating an officer was an offense punishable by death, but returning to civilian life without proper documentation was even riskier. Once again, his situation was precarious.

"I hadn't communicated with my family for months and had no idea how to find them," George said. "Finally, I located an aunt who told me they had moved from place to place, seeking refuge with peasants in return for bribes, only to be evicted whenever their benefactors felt the money was not worth the risk. Although it seemed cruel, it was understandable; because anyone caught harboring Jews was executed."

At her suggestion, he contacted a distant cousin who believed his mother might still be hiding in a villa in Buda.

"I walked up to the door on the pretext of asking for water and who should answer but my mother," he said. "She broke out in a huge smile and was ready to hug me, uniform and all, when I put my fingers to my lips: 'Mrs. Horvath, how wonderful to see you after all these years.' She immediately took my cue and chatted as if I had grown up next door, then led me back into the kitchen where she introduced the odd bedfellows, six Hungarians living alongside two German deserters."

Once again, George's gift for languages paid off when he told the Germans that he, too, had deserted his post. "I told them that the Hungarian army scattered to the wind when we heard that the Allies were coming," he said. "Then I wove a yarn about coming home only to discover that my home had been destroyed in the bombings and I had no idea where my family had gone." As if to punctuate his story, sirens sounded warnings that another Allied air raid was underway and the group took cover in the basement. When they emerged, George pulled out his deck of cards to amuse the ragtag group. One of the Germans was so delighted to have found someone who could not only speak his language fluently but also fill the long hours, he offered to share his room and secret stash of fine Swiss chocolates, a rare delicacy in wartime.

Twenty-five years later, when George owned Custom Chemicals, Inc., an industrial chemical consulting and manufacturing business, he had frequent dealings with a major German chemical company whose U.S. headquarters were in New York. During a business conversation, their vice president, Heinz Schuster, asked George where he had come from originally. When George replied, "Hungary," Heinz remarked that he had been in Budapest during the war. It took only a few moments for them to realize that they had lived in the same villa at the end of the war. Heinz was the German officer who had shared his room and chocolate.

"I suspected all along that you were Jewish," Heinz told him. "But you were a delightful companion and wonderful diversion in difficult times. Deep down, I despised the Nazi position on the Jews and thought many times about deserting because of the atrocities."

Several months later when Heinz visited Atlanta on business, we spent a very pleasant evening talking about these strange coincidences. The unlikely friendship blossomed over the next few years as they continued to conduct business together.

Chapter 4

Until George shared the dramatic details of his escapades and narrow escapes during the war, I hadn't shared mine with anyone, not even in my letters to Dan. I suppose I was afraid that telling the story aloud would bring all the bad memories crashing down around me. But one evening over a steaming plate of *töltött kaposzta* (cabbage leaves stuffed with ground meat and rice in a sauerkraut sauce) at Apostolok — George took my hand. "Eva, I know you and your mother struggled during the war, but I have no idea how you managed to survive. Help me understand."

I hesitated. "You were in Italy in 1941, when all hell broke loose here," I told him. "Long before you returned home, the Germans were like giant boa constrictors, squeezing every vestige of ordinary life from Jews. First came the order to sew those despised yellow stars on our clothing. Next we were told we had to sit in the back of streetcars, even if seats were available in front. Then, they restricted access to our bank accounts so we could only withdraw small amounts of our cash at a time and could not even access our own safety deposit boxes. Mother's box contained my grandmother's heirloom jewelry and some extra cash. We were worried sick that if our funds ran out, we would have no extra funds to pay our way and no jewelry to barter."

Once I began talking, I couldn't seem to stop. I told him about our friends, the Grossbergs, who had emptied their lock boxes before the restrictions and entrusted their valuables to servants. At war's end, they retrieved most everything. Other families were betrayed by servants who either conveniently disappeared or swore that the Germans or Russians had confiscated everything left in their care. We never saw my grandmother's antique jewelry again.

Before long, Arrow Cross soldiers wielding guns stormed into apartments and forced Jews into the backs of trucks. Anyone who disobeyed was shot on the spot. They were then transported to already over-crowded ghettos, housing as many as eighteen or twenty unrelated people in a space once occupied by a single family. Somehow, Mother and I were passed over, but I often peeked through the curtains to watch people herded down the street like cattle. I was furious that they didn't fight back, but I guess they felt any form of survival was better than risking sure death by attacking the guards.

"Soon after, young men like you were ordered to camps along with thousands of others. The first time it touched anyone we knew was when my friend Katalin banged at the door one night, clutching the hands of her two children. She was hysterical. 'They came for Fredek last night,' she sobbed on my shoulder. 'I couldn't do anything to stop them because I was afraid they would harm my babies if I spoke up.' Our hearts were heavy. Although no one uttered the words, we all knew that the haste of the nighttime round up meant that Fredek was on his way to a forced labor camp and her likelihood of seeing him again was slim."

Still, Mother and I seemed safe for the time being — perhaps because I was working in a law firm with both Jewish and Christian partners, or that we had fair complexions and looked more Christian than Jewish. I'll never know. But when my boss was forced out of his own firm because he was Jewish, I left too, assuming I would not be far behind.

I found a job at a factory manufacturing aluminum parts for German war machinery, but it didn't last long. I worked in the chemical area and within a few days, the build-up of fumes caused my eyes to tear constantly. A well-educated but flirty young German guard even brought me eye drops. Though they didn't help much, it was an exceptionally kind gesture toward a Jewess in those days and the two of us developed a quasi-friendship. He would take his post near the area where I worked and talk about many of the things I loved — classical music, antiques, and art. His presence staved off the monotony of performing the same task over and over.

When my eyes began tearing so much I could barely see, I reluctantly quit. Luckily, I found a job as an aid in a Jewish maternity hospital; it ended a few months later when the Germans abruptly closed the facility. In desperation, I approached Lajos Gottesman, a trusted Christian neighbor and attorney, who offered me a job as a domestic at his apartment. Though menial, the job paid enough to supplement Mother's waning income as a language tutor and kept me out of harm's way.

"These are critical times, Eva," Lajos said. "I know you and your mother are struggling. Will you let me help?"

We sat down at his kitchen table as he explained that he was a *sliah*, an agent for the Jewish Underground. "I can have false identity papers made for you and your mother if you promise to leave Pest and take refuge in Buda across the Danube," he said. "As soon as the documents are ready, you must leave your apartment just as it is and disappear."

The decision to leave our apartment was gut wrenching, but there was no other choice. A few weeks later, Lajos came home with impeccable documents, obviously prepared by an expert. Even with my experience reviewing legal documents on a daily basis at the law firm where I had worked, I couldn't detect them from the real thing.

The next day, we tucked our precious new identification papers into the recesses of our pocketbooks, layered on as much clothing as we could, and packed small valises with the essentials. Mother cried when we locked up our apartment, but I was relieved. "At least we're taking some action rather than waiting for the inevitable," I told her.

As soon as we crossed the Danube to the Buda side, I embraced my new identity as Barbara Nagy. "I'm going to dye my hair dark brown and buy some thick glasses so I look bookish," I told Mother.

"I suppose you're right, but I hate it," she told me, putting her hand on my blond hair.

In those days, you couldn't buy hair dye as we know it today, so I mixed a concoction of ersatz coffee, rosemary, and sage I picked from a stranger's garden and rinsed my hair over and over until it turned dark. Instead of wearing it long and loosely curled, I tied it back in an unattractive bun and put on my new glasses. I knew I had achieved my goal when I passed a Christian friend on the street and she didn't recognize me.

Mother and I both found jobs quickly. I took a typing test at a printing company to prove I could type more than one-hundred words-per-minute and was hired on the spot. Mother, posing as Margit Kocsis from Miskolc, a small village south of Budapest, found steady work as a live-in nanny in a high class Christian household.

I had only been working at the printing firm for a few weeks when a co-worker began talking loudly about the "filthy Jew who cheated her." I held my breath the rest of the day, wondering if she had somehow uncovered my secret. As I walked toward my boarding house trying to figure out what to do, I recognized John Kovacs, a young Jewish intern at my old law office. He was dressed in an Arrow Cross uniform. And limping. My first impulse was to get away as fast as I could, but we had run around in the same crowd and I was fond of him. Curiosity got the better of me.

"Is it you, Eva?" he asked. "I hardly recognized you."

Without answering him directly, I gave him a big hug and whispered, "What are you doing in a uniform? You could get shot for wearing that."

He looked so woebegone that I let him lead me over to a park bench. "The risk is even greater if I don't wear it," he said. "I broke my ankle when I jumped from my bedroom balcony during a nighttime round-up and limped the few blocks to my father's grocery store where I hid in the storeroom. The next day, I bribed a greedy school chum with gold coins in exchange for the uniform."

I mulled his story over. Adding together the experiences of so many young Jewish men like Katalin's husband, Fredek, and the fact that Hungarian paper money was nearly worthless, it made sense for a lowly soldier to exchange a uniform for gold coins.

We chatted for a few minutes about the terrible state of affairs in Hungary. When I stood up to go, he grabbed my hand and held it tightly. "I have a proposition for you," he blurted out. "Would you consider living together as newlyweds on a strictly platonic basis? As long as I'm in uniform, I can come and go as I please and as my 'wife,' you will be given the same courtesy. We can tell people that, like so many couples, we decided to get married when I came home on leave, but that I have to return to my unit as soon as my ankle heals."

I was totally taken aback. I knew my mother would tell me that no well-brought up young Jewish woman would consider living with a man she wasn't married to, but war makes strange bedfellows. I also reasoned that, like me, he appeared more Aryan than Jewish and the charade might work. Besides, some plans are short term, others have long-term possibilities with benefits.

"I'll think about it and let you know on Wednesday," I told him. "Meet me back here at the same time." In truth, I had already made up my mind, but how I dreaded telling my mother on Thursday, the one day of the week we always met! There was no doubt she would oppose our wild scheme.

How right I was. She gave a dozen reasons why it was a bad idea and, trying to calm her down, I listened respectfully. Then I told her about my worries at work over the possibility of discovery.

"Even if the scheme doesn't work for long, it will buy me some time to come up with a new plan," I told her. She pressed her lips together, clearly indicating her displeasure, then grabbed me. "Be careful," she said. "He may have a broken ankle, but other parts of him likely work very well. You may have to defend yourself from unwanted advances."

John planned the escapade carefully. He found a tiny room in a boarding house and laid the groundwork with the landlady, explaining that we didn't have time for a church wedding. When we arrived at the apartment the day of the "ceremony," I wore my best navy blue crepe dress and carried a bouquet of flowers. She welcomed us warmly and had even invited other tenants in the building to a small celebration.

During subsequent days, John left the apartment on the pretext of performing duties at headquarters. Until I could secure another job, I stayed in the tiny apartment and played the good housewife, doing laundry in the sink and shopping for decent vegetables and meats every day during a severe shortage. There was just one hitch. With only one bed, we were forced to sleep together and contrary to his promise of a completely platonic relationship, he constantly made sexual advances. I spent nights moving his hands off my breasts and wiggling over so far to the edge of the bed I nearly fell out. Some nights I tried sleeping on the floor. But there was little heat in the apartment and only one blanket between us, so I usually returned to his bed after a few uncomfortable hours, choosing the warmth of another human being over a frigid, sleepless night on the wooden floor.

The arrangement was far from ideal. Though I was bored staying at the rooming house all day being the happy housewife, I was too afraid to seek work. To add to my discomfort, the landlady frequently stopped by on the pretext of getting acquainted. I couldn't decide whether she was just lonely or suspected the truth. I lived in constant fear that John and I would stumble over our concocted story and expose our little ruse. After just a few weeks, I decided to call the "marriage" quits.

My timing was terrible. Daily bombardments made conducting business impossible and one office after another closed. I found myself without a job and barely enough money to pay for room and board at a shabby rooming house.

To make matters worse, I had a narrow escape from two Arrow Cross officers who accosted me on the street, demanding to see my identification papers. I was so afraid that the nasty Nazi sympathizer at my last job had reported me, I felt like a rabbit cornered by a pair of foxes. I hesitated presenting my Barbara Nagy identification since the picture on it didn't match my new persona. But if I didn't, they could shoot me on sight.

I took off the thick glasses, shook out my hair from the tight bun and flirted openly. "Officers, I live right here," I said, fluttering my eyelashes and pointing to the building I was passing. "Let me just run inside and get my identification papers. It won't take a second."

One grabbed me by the arm and whispered, "I'll expect something in return for my trouble." He leaned against the wall and lit a cigarette. His partner followed suit.

"I'll be right out," I assured him as I hurried through the unlocked door, praying they would be more interested in having a smoke than following me. Luck was on my side. The building had apartments on either side of an open courtyard and the unlocked door at the end led to an alley, then all the way through to the next street.

Heart in my pocket, I had to keep reminding myself not to run and arouse suspicion, but I didn't stop until I found a little park blocks away. Though I hadn't prayed in months, I sat down on a bench and recited the Jewish prayer, *"Shema Yisrael adonai eloheinu adonai echad* (Hear, O Israel, the Lord our God, the Lord is One" — Deuteronomy 6:4). Then I put my head in my hands and sobbed.

I ached to share my experience with Mother, but our scheduled time to meet was a few days hence. By then, I had calmed down, buoyed by news on the Underground radio station that the end of the war was imminent.

"Don't return to your apartment," mother said. "While I was taking little Barto for a walk in his pram, I spotted a cellar where we can hide. I think some people may already be there." At that moment, the air raid sirens began screeching and we had to find cover quickly. Frantically, I looked around for the well-marked signs *"Ovohely"* on public bomb shelters. "Follow me," she said. "It's not far."

Anticipation mingled with fear as we walked rapidly through the falling snow toward mother's secret cellar. Hearing ominous footsteps behind me, I glanced over my shoulder. "There's a man behind us," I whispered. "Do you think he's a German soldier?"

"Act normal," she hissed.

My stomach turned to oatmeal as the footsteps came ever closer and I could see mother's right eye twitch, a sure sign she, too, was a basketful of nerves. He brushed beside me so closely his arm jostled my valise, but thankfully, his only interest was finding refuge from the bombings. "How much further?" I asked. "That last bomb was much too close."

Mother led the way down a narrow street to a small house. Even under a blanket of clean snow, it was apparent that the house hadn't escaped the wrath of prior Allied attacks. The front porch was in shards and the roof had portions open to the elements. "It looks on the verge of collapse. Are you sure it is safe?" I asked dubiously.

She shrugged, "What other option do we have?" We picked our way through the rubble toward the rear, nudged the door open and cautiously made our way down a dark stairway into the small dank cellar. A dozen pairs of eyes, mostly women's, locked onto ours, apparently as frightened of us as we were of them. Would they force us to leave after the bombings? The thought terrified me. There were no safe houses for Jews in either Buda or Pest.

But I needn't have worried. The fear in their eyes abated as soon as they realized we were just two more war-weary Hungarians. We scanned our refuge in the semi-darkness. With dirt floors and walls, it was really more a dugout than a basement and the temperature was no warmer inside than out. Some of the women who huddled against the frozen earthen wall had placed barriers of cardboard behind their backs to chase away the cold, but nothing prevented the wind from gusting through the small shattered windows that remained uncovered to make the house appear abandoned.

Hearing no opposition to our arrival, mother and I made our way to the only remaining sitting space, a long bench in the middle of the floor. A lone child broke the ice. "My name is Marika," she said solemnly. "I'm 10 years old. This is my grandmother and those men are

Jakab and Laszlo. Jakab let's us listen to his radio and Laszlo tells me jokes. What's your name?"

I smiled. "I'm Barbara Nagy and this is my friend, Margit Kocsis." When she returned the grin, I knew she was happy to discover new friends. Gradually, others introduced themselves. No one asked if we were Jewish, a fact we would have vehemently denied. I imagine some of the other occupants had the same issue.

Mother and I quickly forged an alliance with Marika's grandmother and the woman sitting on the opposite side and we took turns stretching out on the wooden bench. Marika, who sat between her grandmother and me, put her head in her grandmother's lap at night and I pulled her thin legs onto mine. When temperatures plummeted, we snuggled together as close as a basketful of puppies.

Despite the lack of beds or any creature comforts, we found kinship and remarkable cooperation in our makeshift shelter and felt safer than we had in months. Even the relentless bombardments that pierced the sky were welcome, a signal that the Allies were coming closer each day.

The temperature may have been frigid, but it was far better than braving the elements — and the enemies — outdoors. We rarely lit our meager supply of candles and talked softly to keep our presence secret from the outside world and alternated trips up the rickety stairs to use the toilet, which miraculously still flushed. Laszlo's radio was our one link to the outside world and despite the spotty signal and continual static, we gathered around as soon as he turned the dial. Hearing news of the coming liberation was our lifeline.

Day by day, the bombardments lessened. "The end of the war is near," an elated newscaster reported. "We have reports that the Germans are in retreat and liberation is in sight!" A cautious, but joyous whoop went up from our little band and we celebrated by going outside in broad daylight to loot food from boarded up shops. It felt wonderful to be out in the open and breathe fresh air. As for our mission, I felt no remorse. When you're starving, you don't think of civilities, just filling your stomach.

We met with great success that day, but most of our forages were fruitless and the rumbles from our growing stomachs echoed throughout the night. Occasionally, we would find a meager supply of canned and packaged foods with missing labels, but it didn't matter. We put as many cans as we could carry into baskets, then stuffed our pockets with the overflow. Back in the cellar, we shared a few can openers and utensils and ate right from the cans.

Even though bombardments had become part of our daily lives, the pitiful whinny of a horse in pain, then a volley of bullets, brought immediate terror. Marika curled up in a fetal position in her grandmother's lap and whimpered. One of the women voiced what we were all thinking, "Oh, God, will we be next?"

When Jakab could bear the suspense no longer, he dragged a bench to the window and peered outside. "There's a dead horse in the middle of the street," he whispered excitedly. "If no one comes to claim him, we'll have fresh meat tonight for dinner." Though I had certainly never tasted horseflesh, I salivated at the mere thought of fresh meat. It would be the first most of us had tasted in many, many months.

As soon as the sky darkened, every single person in the basement descended upon the carcass. While several members of the group stood watch, Jakab, who had been a butcher prior to the war, showed us how to dissect the animal. He wielded the largest knife and four of us — including Mother and me — carved out large chunks with the dull kitchen knives as best we could. Others held the baskets, ready to catch every morsel of horsemeat we could scrape out. When Jakab declared our job complete, he carried the two baskets holding the largest pieces back into our subterranean hideout as carefully as if the contents were fine Hungarian Herend porcelain.

Back in the cellar, the mood turned festive. We tossed caution aside and decided to cook the meat on our small Sterno heater, which Laszlo set up near the window. While several women cut the horsemeat into bite-sized chunks and dropped them into the pot of hot water, Mother and I scoured the remnants of the kitchen for spices. We discovered a large pot of salt, a little pepper and a few unmarked jars and generously sprinkled the contents into the pot where the meat was boiling. To our surprise, the most reticent woman in the group pulled out a hand-carved piccolo and played a medley of cheery tunes.

It's odd what hunger does to your psyche. Not a single one of us was repulsed by the thought of eating horsemeat. Instead, we were tantalized by the odor — similar to strong beef. We were so anxious to get a taste that every few minutes someone would stick a fork into a piece to test for tenderness. Even little Marika took a few turns.

The wait was interminable, but our first bite of that succulent meat was far better than the finest filet mignon I had ever eaten. We ate slowly, savoring every bite until our stomachs could hold no more. Then, we packed the remainder in snow so we could make it stretch for a few more days. The thought of having meat again made us feel a few degrees warmer that night.

Two days later when we ran out of meat, we rationed a few cans of sardines and beans, whatever we could find. Before long, our stomachs grumbled ravenously, but we were far too fearful of the departing Germans and the forthcoming entry of the victorious Russians to venture outside again. Rumors were rampant that their leaders allowed three days of looting and mayhem when they liberated a city.

An eerie pall hung over the city and we were on pins and needles, straining at any unusual activity or sound in the street. After the constant bombardments, silence was terrifying.

"Do you think the Russians have arrived yet?" Marika's grandmother asked. "Can we listen to the radio?" Oddly, news was agonizingly sparse. We quietly celebrated the end of the bombings, but bided our time inside, worrying about events yet to unfold.

At daybreak the next morning, our worst fears were realized when three Russian soldiers dressed in full uniform with tall fur hats and heavy black boots stomped down the cellar stairs yelling in Russian. Mother and I huddled so closely together, I couldn't tell who was trembling more; once again, Marika tucked her face under her grandmother's ample bosom and whimpered.

When none of us responded to their orders, one of the Russians cocked his gun and motioned for us to pull up our sleeves to reveal any watches or bracelets. The tallest one pointed his bayonet and motioned for us to take off our coats so he could frisk us. The third went around the room dumping out the meager contents from our valises and tossing everything of value into a large sack. He seemed especially elated when he found bottles of cheap perfume or mouthwash that contained alcohol.

As the soldier doing the frisking inched his way toward me, he spotted the small gold heart locket I always wore, a childhood gift from my parents, and motioned for me to take off my scarf and lift my long hair away from my neck. I squeezed my eyes shut. If he was going to kill me over a gold locket, I didn't want to see the bayonet coming. To my surprise, he removed it as gently as a lover, then, without warning, yelled what I thought must be obscenities and grabbed me firmly by the wrist. I tried to pull in the opposite direction, but his grasp was so firm, I was totally ineffectual. One step at a time, he pulled me up the stairs toward the top. The more I struggled and screamed, the tighter he held on.

"Let me go," I shrieked, first in Hungarian, then in my very minimal Russian. He shouted something in return and, though I didn't understand, Mother knew enough of his language to catch his drift. She sprang into action, knowing instinctively that if he succeeded in getting me away from the cellar, he would likely rape me, then let the others have a turn. She was determined to save me from that grim fate or die trying.

Solidarity among our group quickly dissolved and other than Marika, who was screaming, everyone else stood silently by, even the two men. Before the war, members of a close-knit group like ours would have likely come to my rescue. But Hungarians had long since turned a blind eye to the plight of their countrymen, particularly Jews. Not one person was willing to risk his or her life to save mine. Except my mother.

"Go back," I yelled at her, "Go back before they hurt you too."

Undaunted, she grabbed my free hand and tried to pull me back down the stairs into the basement while screaming hysterically in Russian, "Let her go! Let her go! This is my daughter."

My attacker threw his head back and laughed at the ferocity of my tiny mother's wrath. But by that time, we had reached the top of the stairs and he was dragging me onto the flat landing. Mother held on for dear life, stumbling along behind us. Then, with one swift motion, he yanked me free with such force that Mother careened backwards near the top of the stairs. Other than screaming, hoping the others would come to our rescue, I could do nothing to help her.

I was so intent on our predicament, I didn't hear the other two soldiers come up the stairs. Suddenly, there they were, shouting orders. To my surprise, the brute abruptly released his death grip on my wrist and I sprawled near Mother, who scooped me into the circle of her arms much as she had years before when my father left us for his mistress. "You are safe, my daughter, you are safe," she crooned as the Russians fled.

Mother and I huddled where we were until the roar of an approaching motorcycle spurred us back into the cellar. Maddeningly, the incident was totally ignored by the group, who acted as if nothing had occurred. I bit my tongue to keep from lashing out. I knew my mother's efforts had not only saved me from gang rape, but had likely saved the other women who had cowered in the cellar, unwilling to come to our aid.

Understandably, we lost all our enthusiasm for the group, but we were entering a frightening new historical event. Instead of fearing Hungarians who had turned inexplicably on their Jewish neighbors, then the ruthless Germans determined to exterminate us all, we were obviously going to have to endure the looting and violence of our so-called Russian liberators. Was the worst yet to come?

Chapter 5

On our tenth day in the cellar, a ray of sunshine sliced through the clouds and we felt optimistic enough to discuss departure. We emerged en masse, stunned at the contrast of the outside world. Overhead the perpetually gray sky had turned blue as if in celebration of the liberation, a stark contrast to our bleak corner of the world. Everywhere we turned, we saw devastation. Of the few buildings that stood when Mother and I entered the cellar, few remained intact. The streets were so littered with disabled vehicles and chunks of concrete that the roads were nearly impassible. It was yet another trauma to be endured.

Without a word of goodbye or even a smile to anyone except Marika, Mother and I headed silently toward the Danube while the others drifted every which direction. Their failure to make any move to answer my cries for help had left a bitter taste in my mouth. I certainly had no interest in their destinations. I just wanted to put as much distance between us as possible.

The next hurdle presented itself immediately. From our vantage point high on Buda's hillside, we could see that every bridge connecting Buda and Pest within sight had been destroyed. Our only hope to reach our apartment in Pest was by boat. We picked our way over rough natural terrain and rubble, stepped over discarded household belongings and continued to plod laboriously downhill. When we paused to rest, we added up our resources. We had only a few Hungarian bills which were likely worthless — and thanks to the Russians, nothing of value left to barter for food or transportation. "Don't worry," Mother said, feigning optimism. "We'll find a way. Don't we always?"

When we finally reached the Danube, we spotted a barge a short way downstream that seemed to be preparing to leave the dock. I darted ahead, waving frantically to the boat captain. "Wait! Please wait for us," I screamed. By the time I reached it, I was gasping for breath. "Can you help us get to Pest? I'm afraid we have nothing to offer in return for your kindness."

The elderly barge captain gave me a once-over, taking in my shabby appearance, but his look was totally non-threatening and his brown eyes twinkled behind thick glasses. "No matter," he said. "All are welcome."

Tears of gratitude trickled down my cheeks and I brushed them aside with the back of my glove. "No need to cry, little lady," he said. "You look like you need a helping hand."

Mother and I dropped wearily down on the deck beside other survivors for the short ride across the Danube. As we disembarked, we thanked the captain repeatedly and, on impulse, I gave him a bear hug. "I hope you find what you're looking for," he said. "I'll pray for you." His generosity was so overwhelming at a time when civility had been obliterated from Hungarians that, sixty-five years later, I can still visualize his warm, toothless grin.

Slightly disoriented, we struck out in what we hoped was the direction of our old apartment. It was impossible to get our bearings because while some streets were largely unscathed, others had been eviscerated. There seemed no rhyme or reason to the destruction. Buildings that might have been landmarks were damaged beyond recognition. We were shell-shocked by the evolving panorama and the thought that our beautiful Budapest, once considered a European jewel, was irreparably scarred.

Walking silently for hours, we let our fears about the future swirl in the breeze like broken cobwebs. Would our old apartment still stand? If by some miracle it was intact, how could we reclaim it and our lost belongings if others had moved in?

Between hunger, the mental strain, the weakness of starvation, and the physical toll of living in the cellar, Mother was near collapse. Frequently, she dropped to the ground to rest, her face a blank page. Tears trickled down her cheeks emphasizing the newly formed wrinkles etched in her face. I was glad there were no mirrors nearby. She would have been appalled at her appearance. Likely, I looked no better.

I broke the silence. "We need to come up with a plan in case the apartment has been destroyed or is occupied by another family," I told her.

Mother's eyes flashed and I saw a spark of life for the first time since we'd begun our odyssey. "I don't care if we have to sleep on a street corner," she said. "I'd rather die than demean myself by asking your father and his mistress to take us in."

Painful recollections of myself as a 14-year-old, returning home to find my mother in a state of shock engulfed me. "Your daddy moved out to be with his mistress, Magda, and left us with nothing," she had said. "I don't know how we're going to make it on our own." Her words — and his actions — changed the world as I knew it. I had had to give up my dreams of going to university forever in order to help support us.

"I have no desire to deal with Magda either," I said bitterly. "We'll think of something," But I didn't even convince myself. No matter how many scenarios I turned over in my mind, I couldn't think of a single solution.

As we rounded the corner to our old neighborhood, my adrenalin kicked in and I took off at a run, then doubled back. "Come quickly," I yelled. "It's still standing!"

Spurred on by my words, Mother caught up. We walked the rest of the way side by side, then stood outside for a few minutes trying to decide how to best approach a family who, in our absence, might have made our apartment their own. "We might as well go in," I told her.

"We won't know if we still have a home until we knock on the door."

As we climbed the stairs, mumbled voices wafted through the doors from other apartments, but we could hear no signs of life inside ours. Had the family gone out for the evening or hope against hope, would it be empty? I turned the knob, pushed open the door a crack and called, "Is anyone home?" We were greeted by blessed silence. Still unsure if the apartment was truly empty, I inched the door open a little farther and peered around. To my delight, the parlor appeared totally unchanged and our tired sofa, two chairs and the side tables were in the same positions we had left them a year prior.

Again I called, "Anybody home?" No reply.

Feeling more confident, Mother and I explored each of the small rooms, peeking into empty closets and drawers. There was no food in the icebox. No hot water and no working telephone. But it was ours. I grabbed Mother around the waist and danced her from room to room like a kindergartener, giggling about the missing paintings and rugs. They were mere objects. We were safely home at last!

When our laughter died down, hunger set in. Neither of us could remember when we had eaten our last meal and I flung open a cupboard door, praying that the previous occupants had left something of substance behind. Two lone cans of beans stared back at me, setting me off into more gales of laughter. During our past year on the run, we had consumed more beans than we had in our entire lifetimes, and here we were back in our own apartment, dining once again on beans.

Still giddy over our good fortune, we turned our simple meal into a party by using two of the best looking china bowls and sipping water from chipped wine glasses as if it were Dom Perignon. Though not nearly as tasty as horsemeat, the first meal in our own place went down easily and the ice cold bath that followed was even more delicious.

We were so weary from the alternately heartbreaking and exhilarating day, we decided to head for bed early, but the idea was dashed when we heard the screech of tires just beneath the window. I pulled the drape open an inch and watched in horror as three Russian soldiers climbed out and slammed the door to the building open. The sound of their boots clomping up the stairs was so reminiscent of my nightmare in the cellar that my legs turned to goulash.

Their modus operandi was exactly the same. They barged in without knocking and demanded that we raise our hands and stand against the wall. One rummaged through the drawers, obviously angry to find them empty and a second soldier overturned tables and lamps, looking for God knows what. Terrified, we pressed ourselves against the parlor room wall as tightly as wallpaper and watched helplessly as they held up an object for the others to see, then handed it to the third soldier who opened the window and heaved it down to the waiting truck two stories below.

When a soldier emerged from the bedroom hoisting Mother's prized rocking chair over his head, she bolted from the wall and grabbed his arm. "Please don't take that," she screamed, first in Hungarian, then in halting Russian. "It's worth nothing except to me. My grandfather made it with his own hands."

Either the ogre didn't understand her broken Russian or he didn't care. With a flick of his arm, he flung Mother away from him like a rag doll and hurled her beloved chair out the window. The loud crack when it splintered into the truck was the last straw. Mother plopped down on one of the few remaining chairs and wept. Unfazed, they continued confiscating blankets and pots and pans, along with a threadbare Persian rug. "They're looking for anything they can sell on the black market," I whispered to Mother. After what seemed like an eternity, they left as abruptly as they had arrived, but each time they burst into an adjoining apartment, I winced. Was this nightmare never going to end?

By the next morning, I was able to put the incident aside and move on to more pressing things. There was the matter of no money, no food, and no jobs, but my first priority was finding my father, from whom we had not heard in many months. When Lajos Gottesman obtained false papers for Mother and me, I had begged my father to leave with us, but he insisted that since his lover, Magda Banyasz, was a savvy printing company owner, they would be safe. Furious over his bull-headedness and my inability to contact him without breaking my cover as Barbara Nagy, I cut off all communication.

It had been ten years since Father's desertion, but I always blamed Magda for luring him away from us and harbored hope that he had tired of her and wanted to reunite with Mother and me. As I approached their apartment, which had also survived during the bombings, I prayed that he would open the door and scoop me up in his arms.

Instead, Magda greeted my knock. "I want to talk to my father," I said coldly. "Would you get him? Please."

Gently, she pulled me inside and led me to the sofa. "I don't have good news," she said as her eyes filled with tears. "I've had no contact with your father for many months."

Over a cup of steaming spice tea, she told me an all too familiar story. Like so many other Hungarians, Magda and my father were aroused from their sleep by Arrow Cross soldiers. "They let us take small valises, but we knew we were headed toward one of the German death camps," she said.

The picture she painted made me tremble. "Conditions in the boxcar were horrendous," she said. "It was so crowded there wasn't even room for all of us to sit on the floor at the same time so we took turns. When Mother Nature called and we had to use a bucket in the middle of the car that served as a latrine, a crowd would gather around and turn their backs to provide a modicum of privacy. The stench was so unbearable that we vied for places at the open bay where we could breathe in fresh air."

Her words, told in a flat voice, were so sickening, that I covered my ears and shook my head from side to side. I couldn't comprehend how my refined, self-educated father could endure such conditions. He was so fastidious about his appearance that he wouldn't even help Mother plant flowers because he didn't like to get dirt under his fingernails.

I could feel the bile rise into my mouth and made a dash for the bathroom. When I returned, Magda gently placed a cool cloth behind my neck and handed me a fresh cup of tea with a dash of mint.

"This will help," she said, gently. "Do you want me to continue? We can do this another time." Fearing what would come next, I didn't respond for a few moments, then nodded.

Over the next few hours, she told me that they had observed the train's routine and plotted a desperate escape. "It slowed down long before reaching a station and though it was risky, we decided that would be the best time to make our exit," Magda said. "We planned to lower ourselves over the bay to the ground, one after the other, then rendezvous in the woods that ran along the tracks."

Late that night as the train approached a town, father gave the word. They tiptoed over sleeping bodies and motioned to those still awake to remain quiet. "Your father lowered me over the side and I dangled for a few seconds, too scared to move. Finally, my arms gave way and I let go. I was nearly sucked onto the tracks." She pulled up her skirt to reveal an angry red scar that ran from thigh to ankle, then continued. "Blood was running down my leg, but there was no time to tend to it. The most pressing problem was to stay out of sight under a box car parked on an adjoining track, wait for our train to pass and make a mad dash across the tracks into the woods. I frantically looked for signs of your father. Why wasn't he right behind me? Had he been unable to make it over the bay without help?"

How Magda got through that first night with her injury was something of a miracle. She found shelter in a thicket where she improvised a bandage from her slip and huddled the rest of the night in a freezing drizzle. Father never came. By morning, she was feeling the affects of hypothermia compounded by her injury and knew she would have to make her way back to Budapest on her own. "If the Germans found me, I knew I'd be executed," she said. "I prayed your father had jumped off farther down the tracks and would meet me back in Budapest."

During her arduous journey, Magda hid in the woods by day and traveled by night, staying off the roads as much as possible. If she came near a village, she'd rummage through garbage cans for potato peels and moldy bread. "There were times when I doubted I would survive," she told me. "What drove me was the thought that your father would be waiting for me here."

Magda took my hand in hers and forced me to look. "I haven't completely given up hope. You shouldn't either."

I looked into her eyes, trying to convince myself that there was still a chance he was alive. "Do you think he was injured and is in a hospital somewhere?" I asked. "I don't think I could stand knowing that he died in a death camp."

She put her hand on my knee. "There's a third option," she said. "I was more a realist than your father and long before our arrest I bought some cyanide pills on the black market and made him promise that in the event we were arrested without hope for escape, we would take them. Let's both pray that if he couldn't escape, he swallowed the cyanide pill and died at his own hand rather than in a German oven."

Once I began sobbing, I couldn't stop. Magda tried her best to comfort me, but our relationship had been so adversarial through the years, that even in my grief, I shut her out. Eventually, I composed myself, thanked her, and trudged home to tell Mother. I knew that in spite of her abiding anger toward the two of them, she, too, would be devastated.

More than sixty-five years later, I still think of him daily and pray that someday I will get concrete news of his fate from the International Red Cross. Even in 2008 after the release of additional documents from Nazi Germany, there seemed to be no trace of his death. In my heart, I believe the Nazi records are mute because father died by his own hand on the train. Still, the mystery gnaws at my soul.

~~~~

When I finished telling George my story, I snuggled close, surprised at the relief that washed over me. George gathered me in his arms and stroked my back. "That was a war ago," he said. "We're writing a new chapter together."

Chapter 6

Budapest, 1938

The politics in Budapest just before and after George returned were far from stable. Once victory was declared, the United States, Britain, and Russia assumed joint responsibility for post-war reconstruction of Hungary. It was an unworkable triumvirate. Each tried to avoid stepping on the toes of the other — a rivalry that worked against us. Within a short time, each established its sphere of interest and Hungary fell into Russia's Eastern Bloc. As a result, many of our generation aligned themselves with the Communists.

For a time, it seemed they had made the right choice because scores of young people stepped into influential roles in politics and courts of law. George and his closest friends — as well as Mother and I — were decidedly pro-American and pro-British, which set up an unanticipated scenario, one with near fatal results.

Just weeks after George opened his diplomatic office, two strangers walked in and introduced themselves as security agents. They flashed their badges so quickly I couldn't read them and said, "We need to see Dr. Friedlander immediately." Everyone froze in place.

"Certainly," I said. "I'll see if he's busy. May I tell him who is here?"

I found George on the phone and motioned for him to cover the receiver so I could whisper what was happening.

"Find copies of my credentials and take them the documents," he said. "I think they're in the top drawer."

Nervously, I fumbled through the files to retrieve his original assignment papers from the Italian Minister of Post War Affairs and the International Red Cross, then strode purposefully into the reception area feigning bravado. "Dr. Friedlander is tied up on an important call," I told them. "I trust you are looking for these?" One looked the documents over and handed the sheaf of papers to the second man. Then, they brushed me aside and strode into George's office. "We have some questions for you," the larger man barked. "You must come with us immediately."

George paled. "I'm beginning my official assignment and you are interrupting important work," he protested. "What is this all about?"

Angrily, he put a hand on George's shoulder. "I must insist that you come with me *now*," he said. He turned to me. "Dismiss everyone in the office, yourself included. This office is officially closed."

I looked imploringly at George for direction, then from one stranger to the other. They clearly had the upper hand. "Give me your car keys," the thin one said, thrusting a hand under George's arm and yanking him to his feet. The tall man grabbed his other arm and marched him past the small staff and Italians waiting for assistance. Just before they pushed him out the door into the unmarked black sedan, George called over his shoulder, "Get in touch with my father immediately."

Though the encounter took less than five minutes, it was so reminiscent of our collective war experiences that everyone was stunned. "I'm sorry," I said gently. "As you heard, I've been instructed to close the office. I'll be in touch as soon as I know when we can reopen."

Our Italian clients scattered, but it took a few moments for the staff to close up the files they had been working on and leave. I pulled down the shade, placed a "closed" sign in the window, locked the door and dialed Mr. Friedlander.

My heart sank when his mother answered. "They took George away," I blubbered.

"Who took George away? What are you talking about?" she screamed in my ear. I could understand her hysteria. He had survived three forced labor camps and, unlike the sons of most of her friends, had returned home. Losing him now was inconceivable.

"Two men stormed into the office and put him in an unmarked car," I said. "I have no idea who they are. Please have Mr. Friedlander call me at my shop the moment he comes home."

I retreated to George's office and shoved papers nervously around his desk, then returned to my own office while I waited for the call. Instead, Mr. Friedlander rapped on the door.

There was little I could tell him. The descriptions of the two men fit any number of Hungarians and the car bore no official license plate. I sat mute while he called influential members of his stock exchange, one after another. All promised to make discreet inquiries as to George's whereabouts but none held much hope of a quick answer.

Nearly a week went by before George's father contacted me again. "I have news," he said. "My attorney located George. He's being held at Andrassy Street 60."

"Andrassy Street 60?" I squeaked. I could feel myself hyperventilating. That was the address of the new Hungarian police headquarters, modeled after Russia's infamous KGB, a place so secretive it was known only by its address. Few men who were arrested for questioning were ever heard from again. Even worse, it was rumored that the bodies of those who died as a result of torture or starvation were transported through underground tunnels and dumped into the Danube River. Families never learned their fate.

Despite his own concern, Mr. Friedlander tried to comfort me. "We're going through diplomatic circles and doing everything we can to free him," he said. "I'll ring you up tomorrow." True to his promise, he called the next day and every day thereafter, but there was no news for two agonizing weeks.

Then the phone rang. "A nervous young man, apparently a guard, appeared at our front door this afternoon and gave me a message from George written on a piece of toilet paper," he said excitedly. "George wrote that I should pay the young guard generously for delivering the message and offer more for the next message. He wants me to contact the American consulate immediately."

When we heard nothing back from the consulate, Mr. Friedlander decided to contact his family attorney. He was of little use. "Detainees are not allowed to have visitors or even official legal representation," he told us. "I had hoped all this nonsense would end under Allied control."

Mr. Friedlander tried every angle, made endless phone calls and even bribed a few officials, but there was no further news from or about George for some time. I spent sleepless nights and nervous days worrying about whether we would ever hear from him again — or if we would ever learn of his fate. Mr. Friedlander, whose health was already shaky, began having chest pains from the strain.

Just as we were beginning to lose hope, another messenger delivered a note from George. "I'm being interrogated day and night by my former classmates, people I once thought were my friends," he wrote. "They say my assignment is a cover for spying for the Western powers and seem determined to keep me locked up for years. Tell Eva to request a meeting with Lt. Col. Harry McClain, chief of the Hungarian liaison section of the Allied Control Commission, and ask for his intervention in freeing me. I met him shortly after I returned to Hungary. He's the only one who can help me."

We were initially shocked that former friends had turned on George, but given the reality of the Russians vying for dominance and the reluctance of the Americans and British to interfere, we should have seen it coming. Even more troubling, the Italian government absolutely refused to get involved in what they called "local politics," even though George was in Hungary on the behest of their government.

Somehow, I soldiered on at my little secretarial service, trying to keep the business going. As Mr. Friedlander's health continued to deteriorate, his involvement trickled to a stop. It was up to me to get an appointment with Col. McClain. After repeated calls, I finally got the colonel's assistant on the line. "Col. McClain is an extremely busy man," she told me coldly. "I can't give you an appointment unless I know the nature of the visit."

"It is an urgent matter, one that I can't discuss on the phone," I replied. "It's a matter of life and death."

"One moment," she said, rustling through some papers. She came back on the line. "He can give you fifteen minutes, but only if you come over immediately."

I grabbed my coat and arrived breathless, half-fearing the rude secretary would have a change of heart and bar me from the door. Thankfully, he was much more gracious. "I can't make any promises," he told me, "but I'll investigate the nature of the charges against George and let you know."

Several more excruciating weeks passed. Then, out of the blue on a date I'll never forget — September 23, 1947 — Mr. Friedlander called. "George is on his way home right now," he told me elatedly. "I'll have him call you as soon as he is safely inside our door."

I burst into happy tears, then grabbed Mother and proceeded to waltz her around our little office, "He's free, he's free," I shouted while customers looked askance. I didn't care. All I knew was that my love had been released from what I had feared was certain death. Without waiting for his call, I flew over to the Friedlanders' apartment.

When the slam of a car door heralded George's arrival, his mother, sister, and I lined up at the door as if we were standing in a wedding reception line. Mrs. Friedlander showered him with kisses and clung tightly, but he broke loose to give Klari a quick hug, then grabbed me in his arms. When we finally pulled apart and I got a good look at him, I was appalled at the changes in the robust man who had walked out of his office more than a month before. His skin was tissue paper pale and his clothes hung on his thin frame. He looked at me with the vacant stare of a person in shock. What terrible things had he endured?

Over the next few days, he told us his story in bits and pieces. "They wanted to break me so I would confess to something I hadn't done," he said bitterly. "Except for a lousy bowl of weak soup once a day, there was nothing to eat and they didn't allow me to shower. The interrogations lasted for hours, and sometimes they would take me back to my isolation cell, then wake me up an hour later with more accusations. Their badgering continued for days at a time until I thought I would lose my mind." George put his head in his hands.

"Why would they do this to you?" Mrs. Friedlander asked.

"I think the motivation came from Giovanni Rossi, the man who briefly held my position before I came back to Hungary," George said. "No one ever told me why the Italian consulate replaced him with me, but I have a copy of a letter they wrote asking him to turn over everything he had repossessed from the Hungarian Army — money, official documents and vehicles — to me. His accounting was far less accurate than it should have been. I guess he pocketed most of the money and sold the vehicles either on the black market or to the Russians who whisked them out of Hungary."

The details of his ordeal were chillingly reminiscent of his time in forced labor camps. The same screams in the night. The sound of rats scampering beneath his cot. No blanket to stave off the cold. Putrid water, lack of bathrooms, loneliness and despair.

Then he dropped a bombshell. Despite his fury at the Italian government for not coming to his aid, he planned to return to Rome as soon as the proper documentation could be arranged. "This chapter of my life is over for good," he said bitterly. "I want to return to a place where I was happy and safe."

My head spun. Was this George's way of telling me our affair was over? Even if he wanted me to join him, how could I leave Mother alone to run the shop?

The day after his shocking announcement, I confronted him. "How do I fit into these new plans?" I asked.

He seemed surprised. "Why you're coming with me, of course," he said. "How could you think otherwise?"

It didn't take much convincing. The difficult part was going to be telling Mother, an ordeal I put off as long as I could, cautioning George not to mention his plans.

I thought I had plenty of time to sort out the conundrum, because in post-war days, governments were slow to issue travel documents. I secretly hoped George might change his mind in the interim. But as one month slid into another, he became increasingly apprehensive. "What's taking so long?" he fumed repeatedly. "If I stay in Budapest long enough the bastards will find another excuse to arrest me. I'd kill myself before letting them take me back to Andrassy 60 again."

After several months of biting my tongue and shushing George, I summoned my courage and told Mother about our plans, then braced for her objections. I totally underestimated her histrionics. She screamed, cried, and fired questions at me without waiting for answers. "Why do you think George is serious about marriage?" she fumed. "You've been dating for months and he hasn't ever brought the subject up, has he? What will happen if he leaves you for another woman and you find yourself in Italy with no man and no income? What if you got pregnant?"

I couldn't deny that her doubts were well taken nor that I hadn't harbored many of the same worries — plus a few others, most notably my fiancé, Dan, who had written he was returning home from Ukraine in the next few weeks. His impending arrival gave Mother new ammunition. "What are you going to do now?" she accused. "Does Dan even know you've been dating someone else? What are you going to tell him?"

Over the next few weeks, I spent many a sleepless night. Memories of the love Dan and I shared had faded during the last three difficult years and George had taken his place in my heart. How would I feel when I finally saw him face to face? Would my heart choose Dan or George?

After an evening of love making, I broke the news to George. I had no idea what his reaction would be. Would he try to forbid me from seeing Dan? If so, then what?

He sat up in the bed we shared and gathered me in his arms. "I knew he would come home one day," he said. "I think it's best for me to fade out of the picture for a while and let the two of you get reacquainted. I want you to be certain about us." His generosity was so overwhelming it brought tears to my eyes. If it was calculated to win points, it had done its job.

Dan's homecoming was awkward, something I'm sure he didn't understand. I think he chalked it up to our long separation or to the fact that we were now different people who had come through dark times. One thing was patently clear: he still loved me. I saw it in his eyes, heard it in his voice, and felt his passion when he kissed me.

The contrast between the two men couldn't have been greater. Though both were extremely dashing, Dan was my steady, reliable first real love. George, on the other hand, was a man of the world who had introduced me to the possibilities of international travel, adventure, and excitement. While Dan and I had had a loving but completely innocent relationship totally void of sex, my love affair with George had awakened a passion in me I never knew I possessed.

Each time Dan put his arms around me, I wished he were George. Each time he kissed me, I missed George's intensity. Each time he talked about the future, I froze. There was only one thing to do — confess everything.

Dan beat me to it. One afternoon as we were having espresso and dessert, he took my left hand in his and twirled my engagement ring. "Darling," he said. "I'm afraid you don't want to wear this any longer. I think maybe circumstances in your life have changed and you no longer feel that what we had together is important."

I was dumbstruck, unprepared for his blunt statement. Although I was relieved, I considered denying it to avoid hurting him. But in truth, I had been leading a double life, unable to end one relationship and commit to another. Dan had broken through the wall of indecision and opened the door for me. It was easy to step right through.

We lingered for another hour and had a somber conversation about our separate lives over the past three years. "You were the only thing that kept me alive while I was in the Ukraine," he said. "I lived for your letters. Without them, I would surely have given up and provoked the guards into killing me."

Guilt washed over me. I envisioned his living in that frigid land, working long hours under unbearable conditions, nearly starving. "Oh, Dan," I said. "I'm so sorry. I never meant to hurt you. I think that a combination of the war and the long absence left me vulnerable to another man. I needed to feel young and alive again and to have some passion in my life. George was here and if he will still have me, I plan to follow him to Italy."

"Is he going to marry you?" he asked.

"I don't know," I said honestly. "But I know now that I love him and that I'll follow him wherever he goes."

I pulled off my engagement ring and held it out to Dan who shook his head vehemently. "You keep it," he said. "It will remind you of our happy times together." He stood up, gave me a bone-crunching hug, and then walked through the door for what I thought would be the last time. I never dreamed that twenty-four years later we would rekindle our relationship, despite the encumbrance of spouses and children.

Once Dan was out of sight, I hurried back to the shop. My voice shook as I picked up the phone. "Operator, please give me the Friedlander residence," I instructed.

The phone rang twice before George answered. "It's Eva," I said tentatively. "I've just ended the relationship with Dan."

Without missing a beat, George asked, "What are you doing for the rest of our lives?"

PART II

ROME, ITALY — 1948

Chapter 7

A few weeks after I broke my engagement to Dan, George's father died suddenly of a heart attack. "It was the strain of my imprisonment," he said. "Those damn Communists killed my father."

He was inconsolable for weeks. Even though he had never been very observant, he went to the synagogue every morning to take part in the *minyan*, the traditional quorum of ten Jewish male adults required for certain prayers.

The tragedy only added to George's anxiety. The more time passed, the more memories of his incarceration filled his dreams and exacerbated the paranoia from his forced labor camp experiences. He jumped at every unexpected sound, even a slammed door, and cringed whenever he heard Russian spoken.

In desperation, George contacted Col. McClain and asked if he would once again intercede on his behalf —

this time to expedite a passport. The good colonel complied by writing a letter to the Hungarian authorities stating that he needed George to accompany him to Italy to collaborate on scientific projects. The passport arrived in short order.

"McClain did it again," he said, waving it over his head as he rushed into the shop. "I'll soon be on my way."

I tried to be happy for him, but despite his assurances that we would be together soon, I was apprehensive. Mother's constant complaints didn't help. "I don't hear him making any offers to pay for your trip," she said. "How do you know he won't forget all about you when he sees all those voluptuous Italian women? We've been hanging on by a thread since George's office closed. How can you possibly afford to travel?"

Fortuitously, a month after George left, I was offered a part-time job with the new ambassador to Italy, Dr. Victor Csornoky, a politically ambitious attorney who was the son-in-law of Hungary's Prime Minister, Zoltan Tildy. Not only would the job provide me with some sorely needed extra cash to put aside for the trip, his political connection might come in handy. I could hardly wait to tell George all about it.

Dr. Csornoky and I clicked immediately and became more like confidantes than boss and secretary. One day over an espresso, I confessed that as soon as I could obtain a passport, I planned to join my boyfriend in Italy. Knowing well the difficulty of wriggling through the quagmire of red tape, he looked at me sympathetically. "I can't promise, but I may be able to help if you run into difficulties," he said.

Buoyed by his words, I calculated my expenses: train ticket, new clothes for a warmer climate, plus some extra money to live on until I could find a job. Rampant inflation and the necessity of leaving Mother with a cushion to run the shop made the task daunting.

George and I wrote letters throughout our separation. Or rather I did. Despite his lack of funds and inability to find steady work, he called weekly. "I think I've found the perfect solution to stay afloat," he told me one night. "I've been offered a job as a tour guide."

Though George had been in Rome many times when he was a student at the University of Bologna, he was definitely not an experienced guide. Somehow he convinced a travel agent that he was extremely knowledgeable about the city and that his ability to speak six languages would be a great asset to the company. In short order, he sealed the deal.

"Giuseppe told me I was the answer to a prayer because a British group is arriving tomorrow and he hadn't found an English-speaking guide," George told me. "I'm not eager to rub elbows with damn Brits who are doing everything they can to prevent Jewish refugees from entering Israel, but my landlord is demanding rent money before the end of the week or he'll kick me out."

To refresh his memory from his college days, George talked a friend into driving him around the city, then stayed up most of the night memorizing facts from a guidebook. He knew if he did a good job, he would not only get a fat tip, but endear himself to Giuseppe. His first few tours were so successful, he became known as that "charming Hungarian who can converse in any language" and was in constant demand.

A month or so later when George called, his voice was filled with excitement. "I've been offered a full-time job at the Superior Health Institute," he said, his voice rising. "They've asked me to work with the Nobel Prize winner Dr. Ernst Chain on a delivery method for his penicillin project. The salary at the Institute is paltry, but it's an outstanding scientific opportunity and a prestigious position."

I bounced happily around the office for days. A subsequent conversation was equally exciting. "The American Joint Distribution Committee is offering personal loans to people like you and your mother," he said. "I don't see any reason why you couldn't use a portion for travel expenses."

Mother was thrilled with the possibility of a loan and we filled out the application together. An infusion of money would help the business survive in my absence with enough left over for me to join George. I doubled the time I spent studying Italian from my used Berlitz textbooks, mumbling nouns and verbs as I walked to the office. Even my dreams were sprinkled with Italian idioms.

As it turned out, there was no rush. A year later, I had still made no progress securing travel documents and would likely have remained in Hungary indefinitely if it had not been for intervention by Dr. Csornoky who wrote a letter to the Minster of Internal Affairs requesting a passport for his "head of staff" to open an office in Rome. That did the trick; my passport and visa soon followed.

Even though I was crazed with excitement, Mother remained steadfast in her objections — so much so that our close relationship became strained. Finally, my childhood friend, Edit, brokered a peace pact as deftly as a diplomat. "Eva, after you join George, will you promise your mother that you'll set a time frame for the marriage and return to Hungary if George doesn't come through?" Reluctantly, I nodded my assent.

"Mrs. Dukes, with the promise in place, will you support Eva's move to Italy?"

Mother shrugged her shoulders and sighed so loudly the stray cat who had wandered in for a bowl of milk scurried under the couch. Clearly, she was not pleased, but Edit's diplomacy led to a truce. I could begin packing without the weight of her disapproval.

On the day before my departure, snooty Mrs. Friedlander called. "I've prepared George's favorite cookies, preserves, and goose liver pate for you to take to him," she said stiffly. "You may come by and pick them up before you leave."

"How typical," I complained to Mother. "She must know how busy I am winding things down at the shop and packing. You'd think she would deliver them." Not wanting to risk angering the woman who was likely to become my mother-in-law, I made time to pick up the delicacies, but it wasn't without considerable grumbling.

Mother and I said our goodbyes at home that evening. She couldn't bear seeing me board the train toward an uncertain future and I didn't want her tears to mar my dreams. At the ripe old age of twenty-seven, I was finally going to not only reunite with the love of my life, but live in Rome, my dream city, where I could actually see the wonderful places and art I had studied and admired in textbooks.

Despite all the longing to leave the horrors of the war behind me, my departure came with a large measure of guilt at leaving Mother alone. But once the train pulled out of the station, I tossed the dark memories out the open window and marveled at the unfolding panorama of a world filled with golden wheat fields and sunflowers that bobbed their heads in greeting. We chugged over foothills and mountain valleys, paused in towns I had only read about, and passed through villages too small to appear on the map. I was lost in a euphoric dream that George would meet me at the station, bend down on one knee and propose.

Reality hit when I read the "Entering Yugoslavia" sign and the train pulled into the station. Apprehension sat down beside me as I reached for my pocket book containing my exit visa and passport, plus the precious letter from Dr. Csornoky and clutched it my hands. My visa was limited to a three-month sojourn in Italy. Would the documents hold up to the scrutiny of the border patrol?

Peering nervously out the window, I saw three guards board the train and heard their firm footsteps as they went from compartment to compartment. "Show me your passport and personal documents," one demanded as he shoved opened the door. I glued on a smile and handed him the sheaf of papers while the others rifled through my suitcases.

"You brought winter clothing? Why?" one guard accused. "Your passport is only valid until September. Don't you know that Italy is hot in the summer?"

I had carefully rehearsed this exact scenario, but could hear my voice quiver. "My friend Sophia has struggled to find a job in Italy since the war," I said. "She writes that she has no winter clothing so I'm taking her some of mine. I can't bear to think of her freezing through another winter when I have more than enough."

"How much money do you have with you?" another asked. No lie was necessary. They could not possibly consider the scant amount I had saved as excessive. Abruptly, they left with a warning not to close my suitcases until they returned.

I broke into a cold sweat. Logic told me that they were simply verifying the letter from Dr. Csornoky, but I was not thinking rationally. What if they refused to let me cross the border?

Finally, a lone patrolman returned. "You're cleared to continue on your journey, but don't forget that you must return in three months." As the train chugged out of the station, the relief was so palpable that I felt lightheaded. I was on my way.

When the train pulled into the Venice train station twelve hours later, I immediately spotted George wearing an immaculate white linen suit with a pale blue shirt and striped silk tie, looking even more handsome than I remembered. He scooped me up into his arms and hugged me breathless, then covered my lips with long, deep kisses. For a micro-second, Mother's scowling face interrupted my reverie. "Ah," I thought. "You have no idea how much George loves me."

He held me back at arm's length. "You are so lovely, my Eva. I never doubted this day would come. Come. I can't wait to show you the hotel I've chosen." In the cab, I snuggled close, taking in his spicy aftershave lotion and dreaming of a soft bed and a romantic interlude. It was not to be. I barely had time to unpack a few dresses when his best friend, Delio Mariotti, pounded on the door.

"*Andiamo, andiamo* (hurry, hurry)," he said without greeting either one of us. "We have so little time and there is so much I want to show Eva." He picked up my hand and kissed it. "You are even lovelier than George described. If I hadn't married my own Hungarian beauty, Licci, I would have fought him for your hand."

While George and Delio talked excitedly in Italian, I struggled to follow their conversation. Finally, Delio turned to me and said in Hungarian, "Come, you must have your first gondola ride today. Tomorrow you'll have dinner at our house."

George slipped his hand beneath my right elbow and Delio took my left as they steered me toward the famous canals. I practically floated. "I feel like I'm the protagonist in a Hollywood film," I told them happily.

We glided past the Bridge of Sighs, Doge's Palace, and St. Mark's Basin while George and Delio guided me through history. As the gondolier's rich baritone wafted over the canal, I leaned over and kissed Delio on the cheek and said, "Thank you, thank you both for the most perfect day of my life."

Our three days in Venice passed in a blur of sightseeing and passionate lovemaking. After the year-long absence, we couldn't seem to get enough of one another. Somehow, we would extricate ourselves from our room to stroll through the magnificent churches, museums, and galleries. Then we'd return to our comfortable bed. As we packed for the trip to Rome, we had mixed emotions. We hated to leave the city known as the Queen of the Adriatic, but Rome — and our real lives — awaited.

Chapter 8

George had forewarned me about the miniscule room at the Pensione Michelet Micheletti he had rented, but I admit I was unprepared. We joked that we had to walk sidewise to maneuver between the large wardrobe, a tiny table, and a high double bed, but it wasn't far from the truth. I didn't really mind. I didn't even mind that we had to share the communal bathroom down the hall with other renters.

The one thing I truly missed was a kitchen, made more difficult by the lack of cooking privileges in our landlady's apartment on the main floor. The only exception was that we could brew a pot of tea under her watchful eye. For months, we finagled around the rules by cooking soup or stew on a forbidden hotplate. One night, I wasn't paying close enough attention and, before I knew it, the smell of scalded soup drifted down the stairs straight into the landlady's apartment. She banged on the door and without waiting to be invited, stormed in. "Get rid of that hotplate now or you are out on the street!" she yelled. We tucked it away for a while, then pulled it out — only to be caught again.

Life at the Pensione Michelet began each morning with the bark of a paperboy's "Extra! Extra!" just outside our bedroom window. Those first few mornings, I lazed in bed reliving the night of lovemaking while George leaped up, eager to immerse himself in his penicillin research. Although there seemed to be a number of positions available for someone with my secretarial and managerial skills, my Berlitz Italian was so tentative, I muffed the interviews.

One night I was commiserating with friends over my poor Italian when Erdos, one of our Hungarian friends said, "I learned by spending entire days at the cinema. Why don't you give it a try?"

He was dead serious.

"Do it," George encouraged. "We can practice when I get home at night."

My movie marathon worked. When I couldn't follow the dialogue, I would simply sit through another showing. And sometimes I'd sit through it a second time. Within a few weeks, I became attuned to the rhythm of the language and no longer missed large patches of conversation. I also picked up idioms that it would have taken me months to understand. We joked that if a prospective employer quizzed me on the top movies at the box office, he'd hire me on the spot.

Several weeks into my unorthodox Italian "lessons," George came home bursting with excitement. "The American Joint Distribution Community (AJDC) is looking for multilingual people to help repatriate Jewish refugees who have poured into Italy since the war," he said. "It's perfect for you."

To prepare for my interview at the end of the week, I watched two double features by day and conjugated verbs at night with George. My movie marathon paid off. I was called back for a second interview and a week later, I was offered the job.

On my first day at work, I was a nervous wreck, but once the new job apprehension faded, I, too, hopped out of bed at the newsboy's first "Extra, Extra" and raced George to the communal bathroom down the hall, eager to get to the Palazzo Barberini where AJDC's offices were located. The architecture never ceased to amaze me. Constructed in the mid 1600s by Pope Urban VIII (Maffeo Barberini), the palazzo had dozens of graceful archways beneath three tiers of matching windows. Two staircases – one square-shaped designed by the famed Italian sculptor Bernini and the other an oval spiral by the primary architect, Borromini, are considered masterpieces. Just working in the building made me feel like royalty.

Nonetheless, each time I entered I was keenly aware of the dichotomy between the magnificent structure and the ragtag Jewish refugees from all over Europe who came for help. They mulled about beneath the ancient frescos and gazed at the gilded moldings and carved marble statuary that glistened in the light of the enormous crystal chandeliers. Many self-consciously smoothed their rumpled clothing to appear more presentable amid all this grandeur. From the heyday of Rome through Mussolini's Fascist regime, orchestral music wafted through the halls during state dinners and many a formal ceremony took place. Since the fall of the Axis, the only "ceremonies" were entirely bureaucratic. The spectacular palazzo – a work of art in its own right — serves as the Galleria Nazionale d'Art (Museum of Ancient Art) today.

I took my job of locating countries willing to accept displaced Jewish refugees very seriously. Most had fled their homelands so quickly they hadn't had time to find birth certificates, passports, and marriage licenses – all necessary to emigrate to another country. They were stuck in bureaucratic limbo until I could wrest the documents from countries still in turmoil in the aftermath of the war.

While more than ten-thousand refugees waited for acceptance into new countries, the AJDC provided housing in Bagoli about one-hundred miles away just outside Naples. My two colleagues and I frequently traveled there to talk with clients personally. We also met with them while they were in Rome taking AJDC-sponsored courses in carpentry, dressmaking, construction, cooking, and even hat making to help boost their desirability to host countries.

The most frustrating aspect of the job came when their departure was delayed even though I had amassed an inch-thick dossier that I personally presented to various South American consulates. The process dragged on while I sought housing and jobs, a task both daunting and exhilarating. George never knew if at the end of the day I would be steaming with frustration or elated over a successful placement.

In addition to the satisfaction of working at the AJDC, I formed wonderful friendships with two other Evas, both Hungarians. Nearly every day "the three Evas," as everyone called us, would eat our sparse lunches together in the beautiful Palazzo Barberini courtyard and exchange gossip far more delicious than fresh, crusty Italian bread.

The most frequent target of office gossip was Dalia, a Lithuanian woman who headed the agency. It was widely known that she had arrived in Italy with her husband, but had quickly ditched him to form a romantic liaison with the Polish attorney who was second in command. Every now and then, her poor husband would appear at the office hat in hand and stomp away in short order, his brow furrowed and his eyes flashing. How we would have loved to be flies on the wall during their heated conversations.

The lineage of another co-worker, Olga, was equally titillating. I'm not sure where the rumor got started, but she was purported to be Joseph Stalin's love child – a title she wore as proudly as a mink jacket. Everyone speculated on this interesting tidbit, but we never uncovered the true story.

Happily, I was also quickly accepted into George's crowd. Because none of us had money for entertainment, we routinely strolled down the elegant Via Veneto and stopped to mingle with the fashionable set on the terraces of elegant cafés where we nursed a single espresso for hours. Other patrons apparently found our little group amusing, and if they guessed that we were all displaced persons waiting to emigrate anywhere in the world willing to take us, they didn't seem to care.

One evening, we were arguing about the merits of a particular film when someone stopped by our table and asked for my autograph. I looked over my shoulder to see if someone famous was sitting behind me. "Miss Bergman," the woman repeated. "Will you give me an autograph?" When I explained that I was not Ingrid

Bergman, she huffed away muttering how film stars become too self-important to remember their fans. I couldn't decide whether to be flattered or annoyed. Our gang got a good laugh out of the encounter and explained that the film star and her lover, Roberto Rossellini, lived in a posh apartment not far from the restaurant.

A week or so later while we were seated at the same café, a teenager tentatively approached me and held out a film magazine with Miss Bergman's picture on the cover. "You're my favorite film star. May I have your autograph?" She looked so expectant that I decided to go along with the charade. I smiled my best Ingrid Bergman smile and signed it with a flourish. The mistaken identity was particularly amusing since the star spoke Italian with a Swedish accent and mine was decidedly Hungarian.

Steve and his wife Iren who were hoping to emigrate to Australia, were the only married couple in the group. Although they seemed stable, Iren flirted openly with George. It didn't miss my scrutiny. George didn't encourage her blatant behavior, at least not in my presence, but obviously enjoyed the attention. I laughed her off as just another woman who wanted to live life to the fullest. Perhaps — as with Luba — I should have taken it as a sign of things to come.

George and I spent many languid evenings and weekends alone exploring magnificent Rome. He was a human guidebook, recounting information about Rome's archeology, history, art, jazz, and science, a talent that endeared him to me as well as to disparate groups of well-connected people, including those in the Zionist movement.

I'll never forget the day that Rome celebrated the United Nations declaration of the State of Israel. Jews,

Italians, and sympathizers from around the globe poured out into the streets of Rome in a spontaneous celebration. Musicians and vocalists provided a cacophony of music as we danced and sang with strangers. George charmed his way into an advantageous position so we could mingle with the top echelon, but rich or poor didn't really matter that evening. Manual laborers and diplomats, royalty and refugees all celebrated together until the faint glow of a summer dawn lit up the sky.

A few weeks later, an engraved invitation arrived from the Israeli consulate inviting us to a gala celebration at the Hotel Excelsior. "Imagine how lucky we are to be in this very city at this time in history," I told George, excitedly. "The war seems so far away, doesn't it?"

As soon as the words were out of my mouth, I regretted them. Any discussion about the war sent George retreating into his nightmare and he would begin his ritual of double locking all the doors, pulling down the shades and lining up his shoes and mine beside the bed, in case we had to flee in a hurry.

I tried to bring him back into the present. "What on earth will I wear?" I whined. "I don't have the proper clothes for such a grand occasion."

George continued with his mental checklist, but paused long enough to say, "How about that polka dot outfit you wore the day you arrived in Venice? You looked so ravishing that Delio fell instantly in love with you."

I pulled the sleeveless dress and jacket out of the closet and held it up for him to see. "You really think this would be all right?" I asked. "I don't want to embarrass you."

"No matter what you wear, you will be the most beautiful woman there," he told me. His flattery worked. I didn't realize until the next day that he had totally derailed my campaign for a new dress.

Actually, my attire sufficed nicely. Although the wives of the diplomats wore couture gowns probably purchased on the Via Condotti — Rome's equivalent of New York's Fifth Avenue — other women wore street clothes similar to mine. Once again, George's charm and savoir faire launched us into a circle of diplomats and foreign dignitaries discussing Israel's tenuous future. "The fight is far from over," they all agreed. "If the Arabs join forces, we're in for the battle of our lives."

The most difficult moment during our time in Rome came when I found out that we had conceived a child. I agonized about whether to carry the baby to full term or have an abortion. Although we were wildly happy together and both had steady jobs, our situation in Rome was uncertain. Money was always tight and we had no assurance that the Italian government would let us remain in Rome indefinitely. Every six months refugees had to renew their visas, a task fraught with tension and possible deportation. How could I raise a child in such an environment and without the blessing of marriage? We talked about nothing else for several weeks, but in the end, we made the difficult decision to abort the child.

Oddly — even in this Catholic country – abortions could be obtained. George found a well-respected doctor and I had the procedure in his office. As much as I wanted a baby with George eventually, I felt in my heart that this was neither the time nor the place.

I longed to tell Mother about the abortion, but didn't want to worry her or add credence to her mantra about the lack of a legal union. Each letter from her ended with the same postscript: "When are you and George getting married?"

I was beginning to wonder myself. The year anniversary of my arrival was drawing near and my promise to her weighed heavily on my conscience.

"You know that I gave her my word that I would return to Hungary if we weren't married by the end of the first year," I told him. "I can't go back on it."

George was dismissive. "What does it matter?" he said, taking me into his arms for a little foreplay. "We're together. That is all that counts."

"It matters to me. How do you think it makes me feel to be living with you with no thought of making the arrangement permanent? I blush when people call me, 'Mrs. Friedlander' because it's embarrassing to correct them. Do you really love me or am I just one of the many women you've loved and left?"

After weeks of wrangling, he finally agreed and once he made up his mind, he was determined to do it right. "We have to ask the oldest, most reputable rabbi in Italy to marry us," he insisted. "*Our* ceremony can't be performed by just anyone."

Personally, I didn't really care who married us. The Italian equivalent of a Justice of the Peace would have been fine, but I admit that I was thrilled he had become so involved in the process. Eagerly, we approached the chief rabbi in Rome who, much to my shock, readily agreed. However, there were steps we needed to take prior to the ceremony. One was my having a ritual bath at the *Mikveh*, a special bathing pool for women that represented an immersion into Judaism.

Mother was delirious at the news, but at the same time heartbroken that she couldn't attend. Not only did she lack a passport and visa, she had no one she could entrust with running the shop. George's mother, still grieving after the death of his father, decided not to make the journey. She grudgingly called to offer left-handed congratulations. In the most cordial tone she could muster, she said, "My dear, I'm delighted. You are so fortunate to have found a man like my son. I hope you will be the kind of wife he deserves." It was hardly the congratulatory call I wanted from her.

Klari's call was just the opposite. "Welcome to the family, Eva. I'm so excited to have a sister. You're the best thing that has ever happened to George!"

If Mrs. Friedlander was cool, our eclectic crowd made up for her lack of enthusiasm. No one expected a wedding extravaganza. After all, they were also living hand to mouth and understood that the event would be low key. Somehow, George again derailed my desire to buy a new dress and I wore the same polka dot frock that had become my special occasion dress.

We invited only a few close friends to the August 23, 1949 ceremony at the synagogue. The rabbi conducted it totally in Hebrew, a language neither George nor I fully understood. Later he translated it for us in Italian. The sentence that resonated with me most was from Genesis 2:24:

"For this reason a man will leave his father and mother and be united to his wife, and they will become one flesh."

Afterward, George whispered in my ear, "You are my chosen life partner and I will cherish you always."

I hugged him tightly as tears dotted my cheeks. "You will always be the only one I love."

During our wedding dinner at a Hungarian restaurant on the shores of the Tevere River, our friend Charles raised his glass of wine. "To love, to Rome, to America and to eternal friendship," he said. *"L'chaim* (to Life)!"

George lifted his glass in answer, "To the friends who have become family. Wherever the future takes us, you will forever be in our hearts."

~~~~

Once I was officially Mrs. George Friedlander, Rome took on an even rosier glow. At George's suggestion, I enrolled at the Accademia di Belle Arti where I attended classes in art history and art appreciation. I soaked up every word and spent hours in the school library pouring over decorative arts books and visiting museums where so many ancient treasures had survived for centuries.

One of my biggest surprises in Rome was the marvelous Italian system of education which seemed far superior to Hungary's where only the upper echelon were taught to read classical literature or study art and music. Romans, on the other hand, all seemed familiar with the famous operas and revered the divas much in the same way Americans idolize celebrities today. Even the cleaning woman at our little pension sang arias while she scrubbed toilets and mopped floors.

George didn't especially enjoy opera, but he willingly took me to the open air performances in the Terme di Caracalla where I sat transfixed as the powerful voices reverberated through the night sky, enhanced by the natural acoustics of the stark ruins. Whenever I turned to take his hand during a particularly romantic scene, I usually caught him making funny faces at me. Despite the seriousness of the plot, I could barely contain my laughter.

Although we both loved our work, we were constantly seeking new ways to supplement our meager income. Fortuitously, we were introduced to Clara Vertes, an elegant Hungarian woman who lived in a palatial apartment with her charming deadbeat son and a loveable pet boxer named Pluto. She, too, was looking for a business opportunity and best of all, she had money to invest. Our job was to come up with some ideas. It was a partnership made in heaven.

We tossed around ideas for several weeks, but none hit the mark until George suggested that we open a combination spa and beauty shop in a posh area. "You put up the money, I'll formulate the products, and Eva can manage the shop."

"Dahling," Clara said in her Zsa Zsa Gabor voice. "It's brilliant! Eva, you must find us a location near the Spanish Steps and the haute couture shops where the beautiful people gather. And George, use your brilliant scientific brain to dream up divine lotions," Clara added.

We talked late into the night, throwing out suggestions for packaging and décor. In a stroke of luck, I found the perfect spot – a pleasant shop located just steps away from the Via Condotti and around the corner from the former residence of the poet Lord George Gordon Byron. We named our little establishment Centoundici (111) and George designed a classy gold logo for the white square glass jars with black tops. To show them off in the elegant reception area, I found a handsome display case that complemented the Louis XV chairs and Persian rug borrowed from Clara's apartment. The treatment rooms were equally well appointed.

Once the decorating was complete, Clara left the staffing to us. I quickly engaged the former royal beautician for the Queen of Romania, who was highly recommended by our friends, as well as a receptionist/facial therapist who had previously been the proprietor of an upscale Hungarian beauty institute.

The shop's location was so advantageous that I had no difficulty promoting it to nearby hotel concierges who recommended us to their guests. Instantly, we had a stream of clients and a steady income stream. To further promote the business, George used his photographic skills to take pictures of me having a facial, which we used in our advertising.

The only sour note in the business arrangement was the acrimony between Clara and the staff. Since I had hired them, they took directions from me, but she constantly ordered them about while I was at work and found fault where none existed. My skills as negotiator were called into play time after time to assure the staff that their jobs were not in jeopardy. George's task was to soothe Clara's ruffled feathers.

Though our dream to emigrate to America didn't dissipate, we turned down official offers for visas twice. George was determined to be the first scientist on Dr. Chain's team to come up with a viable delivery method for penicillin and the famous chemist often singled him out so they could work together after the others left. My work with the AJDC was equally satisfying and I was just as committed to seeing it through since there seemed no end to the long line of displaced persons needing assistance. We were also delighted with the success of Centoundici since it practically ran itself.

A year after it opened, George and I received our final notice that if we refused the visas to America a third time, we would permanently relinquish our opportunity. It was a gut wrenching decision. Added to our hesitation to leave rewarding jobs mid-stream, I was just six months shy of a degree at the Accademia and I hated to leave the city that had brought me so much happiness for three years. Yet, how could we turn down our dream to live in "the land of opportunity?"

When our documents arrived in the mail, we were shocked that our routing was through New Orleans rather than New York and that our final destination was Atlanta, Georgia, a city we knew little about. "I wanted my first glimpse of America to be the Statue of Liberty and skyscrapers, not some southern city," George grumbled. But after much discussion, we decided that since we had no family or formal sponsorship, it was better to begin our life in a smaller city where we could embrace our dream of becoming American citizens.

We reluctantly told Clara our decision, then boxed up a large supply of George's lotions and bottles with the intention of duplicating the shop in America.

Years later when spas became the rage for the wealthier set, George lamented, "We could have, should have opened a shop shortly after we arrived." It was the first of many goals he never accomplished.

PART III

ATLANTA, GEORGIA — 1950

Chapter 9

Our departure from the Eternal City was more difficult than I ever imagined. Despite the delicious promise of America, the bitter taste of leaving our families and moving five-thousand miles away lingered. I hadn't seen Mother in three years and our tearful conversations left me guilt-ridden. How many more years would pass until I would see her face-to-face again?

On the day before we were scheduled to leave I was struck by such a deep malaise that I didn't think I could make the trip. Pista and Agnes Herman dropped by to invite us for a farewell dinner and found me sitting on the bed staring at my empty suitcase. "I don't want to leave Rome," I wailed. "I love it so."

"Don't be silly," Agnes said. "This is the opportunity you've dreamed of all your life." She walked over to the closet and began folding our clothes. "I'm going to pack your clothes and George's belongings separately. It will make it so much easier to find your things."

I couldn't just sit by and watch her do all the work, so I reluctantly rose and at least made some motions of packing. We had so little that before long, everything except our last minute items had been secured. "We're taking you out to dinner one last time," she said. "You can't refuse."

The next morning before dawn they knocked on the door again. "It's time," Agnes said. "There's no turning back."

As the sun rose over Rome, the train pulled out of the station, and I pressed my nose against the window for a last, lingering look. Tears coursed down my cheeks. George let me mourn for an hour or so, then pried me out of my reverie with chatter about the two-week Atlantic crossing ahead of us. Neither of us had ever been aboard a ship before and we were admittedly apprehensive.

Our arrival in Bremerhaven, Germany, was less than ideal. "Ah, yes, Mr. and Mrs. Friedlander," the bureaucrat at the immigration office told us. "I have your food and lodging vouchers right here. Your ship, the SS General Harry Taylor, will depart on November 12. Enjoy your holiday in our beautiful city."

We were stunned. November 12 was two long weeks away and we were stuck in Germany, a country where six-million Jews had perished at the hands of the Nazis. Was it safe for us even now?

Immigration services divided immigrants among the small, modest hotels that dotted the city and we tentatively settled in, hesitant to venture onto German soil. By the third day, George announced, "I can't stand staying in this room another day. What harm will come from a short walk near the hotel? If Immigration thought Jews were in danger, they never would have sent us here."

To our amazement, we were greeted by friendly nods and, with George's polished German, we had no problem conversing with the proprietors of the antique shops that had sprung up since the war. We repeated the same routine each day, strolling along the quiet residential streets window-shopping or going in and out of shops we could ill afford. Mid-afternoon we splurged on an espresso at a snug café where we lingered until dinner. Occasionally, other passengers joined us.

On our last day in Bremerhaven, I spotted a tiny cut crystal vase in a charming little antique shop on Brübach Strasse. "Look how it glistens when it catches the light," I said. "Do we dare buy it?" George nodded his consent and we approached the shop owner and asked the price. Likely because sales were paltry that day, or we looked so pitiful, he sold it for a pittance and I walked out clutching the object that bridged our lives between Europe and America. Though I own many magnificent antiques today, I still treasure that tiny vase which symbolized my departure from my old world and entrance to a new life.

Bright and early the next morning, we headed for the dock, excited to begin our journey. We hadn't expected a luxury liner, but the dowdy gray troop transport ship loaned to the International Refugee Organization barely looked sea-worthy. Neither did the parade of refugees dressed in bleak black and gray clothing who seemed to melt into the hull of the ship.

"Do you think that the decrepit SS General Henry Taylor is sturdy enough to get us all the way to America?" I asked George.

"You don't think the Americans would want to drown the citizens they've invited to their country," he teased. "It wouldn't be very good public relations."

I wasn't convinced.

My heart sank further when they told us that men and women slept in separate areas instead of individual cabins. Suddenly, all the reasons we had been so anxious to emigrate evaporated. "We should have stayed in Rome and applied for Italian citizenship," I said. "There we had jobs and friends. Who will help us in America if we need it?"

I heaved a sigh and fell into line behind a group of women struggling to manage their suitcases down a narrow flight of stairs. The next shock was the first sight of the large dormitory-style room where we would be sleeping for the next two weeks. Instead of bunk beds, there were rows and rows of double-decker rope hammocks suspended from the ceiling. They were hung as closely together as eggs in a carton and as I sat on the edge of a lower hammock, it rocked alarmingly. The shower stalls were open along the front without a semblance of privacy.

"I thought I'd never have to sleep away from my husband again," said Alzbeta, a Czech woman who had spent nine months in a Russian forced labor camp. I nodded in agreement.

Our first night at sea was ghastly. The ship rocked so violently in the rough November waters that at least half the women — including poor Alzbeta — became violently seasick. Thankfully, my stomach behaved, but how I longed for George's strong arms around me. I learned the next morning that he had been among the most ill of the men and wouldn't be joining me for breakfast. As it turned out, he rarely came to meals the entire trip.

To make matters worse, the captain forbade us from going up onto the deck because of the high winds and crashing waves. One seasick young Pole disobeyed, hoping that fresh air would relieve his nausea. No one missed him for a time. Finally, a friend became nervous and alerted a crew member who found him sprawled out on the deck unconscious. The crew surmised that he was likely thrown by a huge wave and hit his head. The poor fellow died the following day.

The unsettling news spread like wildfire among the passengers and underscored not only the fragility of life, but the enormity of our decision to emigrate to America. Not a day went by that I didn't question my choice to leave Rome.

A few days later, the storm abated briefly and the captain allowed everyone back onto the deck for the young Pole's burial at sea. His friend tearfully read the eulogy and told moving stories of survival during German occupation. It seemed so unfair that just as this young man was on the brink of realizing his dream, his life had been snuffed out.

I'm not sure how it came about, but George and I were assigned as group leaders, responsible for preparing dossiers for more than three-hundred refugees to expedite the immigration process once we reached the port of New Orleans. Even with two of us working together, it would have been daunting, but with George out of commission for most of the trip, the entire task landed in my lap.

To my surprise, the assignment turned out to be a Godsend and kept my mind occupied during the long, choppy days when few people had yet to find their sea legs. Amassing the documents was not dissimilar from my work in Rome and the bursar I worked with had done the same job many times. We worked well together and he introduced me to many of the officers who were happy to help me polish my English.

As an introduction to Thanksgiving, the ship's cook had planned a typical American feast, but with so many still seasick, he decided that steaming pots of turkey soup would be more appropriate. My stomach, on the other hand, longed for solid food. I was thrilled when the captain invited me to join the officers and crew members for turkey, dressing, and all the trimmings. How delightful to hear the story of that first Thanksgiving in 1621 when Pilgrims and Indians shared in the fall bounty. Their story of sixty-five days aboard the Mayflower, a ship far less seaworthy than the SS General Henry Taylor, and hardships in the wilderness, made me feel ashamed of my grumbling. My only regret was that George was still far too seasick to share in the occasion.

The seas calmed down during the last few days of the voyage and even those who had been sickest began excitedly preparing to dock. George finally emerged — pale, thin, and ravenous — eager for a solid meal and the first glimpse of New Orleans. We sailed up the mouth of the mighty Mississippi River, through lush marshlands dotted with small communities and into the New Orleans port. Even though the bursar and I had done our best to expedite the paperwork, being processed through immigration took far longer than anticipated and we didn't have time to tour this lovely city. In fact, we scarcely had time to make it to the train station for our overnight trip to Atlanta. With us were five suitcases stuffed with all our worldly possessions and a grand sum of two-hundred dollars.

Our arrival in our new home in Atlanta twelve hours later was inauspicious. Atlanta was still a small southern city in November of 1950 with none of the New York-style skyscrapers George craved. "All I know about Atlanta is the Ku Klux Klan, Coca-Cola, and *Gone With the Wind*. Is this all there is to downtown?" he asked the cab driver.

"Yes, suh," the cabbie said in that soft southern drawl I loved immediately. "That there is our state capitol. The dome is made from real gold from the Dahlonega mines."

I was mesmerized, but George was unimpressed. He was even more dismayed when we pulled up to the entrance of the Southland Hotel on Ponce de Leon where reservations had been made for us. It looked fine to me, but George had set his sights on more elegant surroundings in the Land of Opportunity. I smiled. Was he expecting the streets to be paved with gold?

We dragged the suitcases up to our clean, neat room with a private bath, dropped them in the center of the floor and fell into an exhausted sleep. Fourteen hours later, the shrill sound of the phone interrupted our dreams.

"Welcome to Atlanta," a female voice said cheerily. My name is Herta Sanders and I'm a volunteer at the Atlanta Jewish Federation. Rest up today and take a look around your new city. I'll pick you up in the morning to look for an apartment."

We groggily took stock. "When did we eat last?" George asked.

"I can't even remember. I guess it was lunch onboard the ship." I grabbed my chenille robe, padded barefoot to the window and raised the shade. "Come look," I said. "There's a small diner across the street. Let's get dressed. I'm starved."

Within ten minutes, we were sitting at the counter salivating over the scrambled eggs sizzling on the grill and sipping cups of steaming hot coffee as we waited for the toast to pop out of the toaster. We ate our first breakfast in America seated in the shadow of a huge billboard advertising the Reverend Billy Graham's upcoming crusade. This was, indeed, a land of opportunity where all religions were tolerated and anything was possible.

Chapter 10

True to her word, Herta knocked on our door the next morning promptly at nine o'clock, and by our third day on American soil we had rented an inexpensive apartment with a sunny living room facing the street, a small kitchen and breakfast room, one bedroom and, luxury of luxuries, our own bathroom. Compared to the tiny pensione in Rome without kitchen privileges, this was palatial. We had taken our first steps toward living the American Dream.

"You're not to worry about furnishings," she said. "The Federation will provide the basics." Though far from fancy, the donated second-hand furniture turned our little place into a home and a parade of women on the Federation's immigration committee bustled in and out, bringing armloads of pots, pans, vases, sheets, towels, and even pictures they had amassed. "This is far more fun than a bridal shower," I told them. "Every day is like the first day of Chanukah."

Herta's next mission was to help us find employment. "George, why don't you call the personnel department at Emory University to set up an interview for a research position? I've heard that they're always on the lookout for brilliant researchers like you." Her praise gave him the push he needed. Within a few weeks he was offered a job at the medical school in the department of biochemistry, where he researched growth hormones. I went on only two or three interviews before being hired as the secretary for the new vice president of Puritan Chemical Company. When we called Herta with the news, she said, "I've never seen newcomers integrate themselves so fast into America," she said. "You've done me proud."

I have to admit, we were pretty proud of ourselves. "Life is even better than I dreamed," I wrote Mother. "We've made so many wonderful friends and the young executives at Puritan even drive me to work every day."

"I'm thrilled for you," Mother wrote back. "Enjoy your new life in America and don't worry about the secretarial service. I've found some new clients that keep us busy." I breathed a sigh of relief, my guilt assuaged for leaving her alone to manage the business.

About six months after we settled in, George was approached to interview for a position doing medical research at Stanford University. He flew to Palo Alto and was offered the job, but they were unwilling to pay for our relocation so he backed off. Years later when the team he would have worked with made a significant breakthrough, he regretted not seizing the opportunity. In reality, it would have been impossible from a financial standpoint.

Over the next six years, we built a life around work and friends. George's research was definitely not as fulfilling as working with Dr. Ernst Chain, so at lunch he would walk over to the Yerkes Primate Research Center located next to his lab and amuse himself by squirting the monkeys with a water pistol. He loved watching them jump up and down in their cages and hiss. "I hissed right back," he confessed.

We repeatedly discussed his return to medical school and he went so far as to talk to the dean of admissions, who assured him that with his credentials, he would have no problem getting accepted. Yet, every time I brought it up, George made one excuse or another. "We're still getting our bearings in America. How can I afford to quit my job to go to medical school? Medical school doesn't end with graduation. You have to factor in years of internship and residency." In the end, he never took the plunge — and it was one of those "could of, should of" opportunities he regretted.

After several years at Puritan, I left for a better paying position as office manager at the Council of Jewish Federations and Welfare Funds. The small one-man office was located in the Hurt building in the center of downtown. My boss, David Zeff, was the regional director and traveled nearly every week, which left me in charge of day-to-day operations. It also left me some free time to take my sack lunch to the Atlanta Library where I poured over antique and art books in preparation for my next career move as a self-employed art and antique dealer.

David was an ideal boss and an exemplary human being. A staunch Democrat and activist, he taught me so much about American politics, the polar opposite of anything I had experienced in Hungary, a totalitarian country. "The strength of our form of democracy is its flexibility," he told me. "Countries under absolute rule are bound to fail." It was as true then as it hopefully is today.

In turn, I told him about my experiences in Rome working with the AJDC, which was similar to the mission of the Council. Instead of working with individual clients, David supervised Jewish organizations in the Southern region and counseled them on how best to run their offices and manage their educational facilities and nursing homes. He was a fascinating man, much like George, who had a broad range of knowledge on multiple topics. The two got along famously.

By 1955, we had been in America for five years and had just become citizens. Both of us were employed and had a comfortable roof over our heads — something we never took for granted. Time seemed ripe to start a family. My biological clock was clicking loudly and I knew because of the extreme malnutrition I suffered during the war, it might be difficult.

When I finally got pregnant after eighteen months of trying, George was thrilled. "Our first will be a boy, and then we'll have a baby girl," he said. Both grandmothers were delighted too. The only thing that marred our happiness was that neither could be present to see our first baby enter the world because Hungarians were still not able to obtain exit visas and passports.

Just prior to Lewis's birth, I resigned to become a stay-at-home mom, but our friendship with David didn't end. He and his wife were frequent guests in our home, and if the two men found themselves in New York on business at the same time, they made a point to get together at a soup café they both loved.

By this time we were living in an elegant coach house on an estate once owned by Coca-Cola magnate Robert Woodruff that was near enough to the Emory campus for George to walk to work. But when George left Emory to take a better paying job at Momar, a leading industrial chemical company, we were in a financial position to buy a home, the culmination of our American dream. George contacted a realtor and asked friends and colleagues to keep their eyes open. A few weeks later, his friend Frank McFall called.

"I found the perfect house for you on Wadsworth Street not far from us," he said. "You'd better come see it quickly. Houses in this area don't stay on the market long."

George made an appointment with a realtor the next day and then took me to inspect the three-bedroom, one-and-a-half bath house on a tree-laden street. "It's perfect!" I told him. "I can plant a garden near the fence and there's plenty of room for a sandbox for Lewis."

We signed a contract so hurriedly that we miscalculated the closing costs and a few days beforehand, we still didn't have enough money. "I guess I'll have to ask Momar to give me a short-term loan," George lamented. "We should be able to pay it back quickly."

The next day, I bit my fingernails until he called. "Relax," he said. "They were very generous and we've worked out a repayment plan." On the day of the closing I was all nerves. The prospect of owning a house with a yard was something I never imagined in Budapest where only very wealthy people lived in individual homes. Most, like Mother and me, lived their entire lives in rented apartments.

Just before we entered the lawyer's office, George pulled me aside. "For your protection, I've asked the attorney to put the deed in my name alone."

I shrugged. What difference did it make? In my mind, what was his was mine and vice versa. It wasn't until years later after I had embraced the concept of women's equality that I learned he had pulled the wool over my eyes. I seriously doubt he had any ulterior motives to cheat me out of my fair share. It was more about his need to control all aspects of our lives, particularly finances, a source of irritation and many arguments once I established my own career.

Our idyllic life came to a screeching halt that October when horrific images of the Hungarian student revolt flashed across the television screen. A peaceful protest over the Soviet's refusal to pull out of Hungary after the election of a new free government turned ugly when students tore down a bronze statue of Stalin and dragged its severed arms and legs through the streets. The last straw for the Russians came when mobs gleefully cut the hated hammer and sickle from the Hungarian flag.

The Hungarian revolt to reclaim the country ended abruptly when President Dwight D. Eisenhower — fearing retribution from their former allies — refused to grant diplomatic recognition to the newly formed democratic government. That gave Nikita Krushchev, then First Secretary of the Soviet Union's Communist Party, tacit permission to use force to squash the uprising. He ordered two-hundred thousand heavily armed troops to fire on unarmed students in the streets. It was a blood bath. The fierce battle ended twelve days later; in its wake, three-thousand revolutionaries and Soviet soldiers lay dead.

As news of twenty-six thousand arrests and twelve-hundred executions continued to fill the airwaves, we feared for the safety of my mother and George's mother and sister, Klari. Hundreds of thousands fled Hungary and crowded embassies in surrounding countries, all seeking visas to emigrate to any country willing to take them. We were frantic, helpless. Then, in an extremely generous gesture, our friend Fred Baumgarten offered to loan George money to fly to Vienna in the hopes of making arrangements to smuggle our families out of Hungary.

George made immediate reservations to fly to Vienna where he camped out at the American embassy, hoping for a chance meeting with then Vice President Richard Nixon. Ironically, after Ike's refusal to step into Hungarian politics, the President had sent Nixon on a fact-finding mission to study the economic issues facing Austria as a result of the enormous influx of refugees and to offer financial and medical aid. Ike also wanted his Vice President to assess the number of refugees America should prepare to receive.

Never one to miss an opportunity, George worked his way toward the Vice President with the gift of a "blood" orange from Israel, hoping the gesture might lead to intervention on our relatives' behalf. It was not to be. Just as it seemed that George had succeeded in finding a smuggler to get our little group across the border into Austria, Klari came down with the flu, which turned into pneumonia. Mrs. Friedlander refused to leave her behind and my mother followed suit, believing the worst was over. The only good news that came from his trip was that my dear friend, Edit, had managed to get a visa to Caracas, Venezuela, where she hoped to begin a new life.

After George returned, we settled back into a routine. George went to work every day and I was content to be a stay-at-home mom and become more active at Ahavath Achim Synagogue (The AA). Out of the blue, we received a letter from the Daughters of the American Revolution (DAR). "Dear Mr. and Mrs. Friedlander," I read. "I'm pleased to announce that you have been awarded the Americanism Medal for naturalized citizens who have made outstanding contributions to our American way of life. At the ceremony in your honor, we would like for you to recite the Emma Lazarus poem carved into the base of the Statue of Liberty, 'The New Colossus.'"

That evening, I showed the invitation to George. "What do you make of it?" I said. "Do you think this organization is legitimate?"

"Why don't you call Herta?" he suggested. "She knows everything about Atlanta."

Our mentor gushed, "How wonderful! The DAR is a very old, prestigious national organization and I don't ever remember a Jewish couple being honored. I'm so proud of you both."

My voice quivered during my recitation at the ceremony, but thankfully I remembered all the words. They seemed to be written just for us.

> *"Give me your tired, your poor,*
> *Your huddled masses yearning to breathe free,*
> *The wretched refuse of your teeming shore.*
> *Send these, the homeless, tempest-tost to me,*
> *I lift my lamp beside the golden door."*

Afterwards, we were surrounded by well-wishers: Herta, grinning like a proud mother, representatives from the Jewish Federation, so many of our friends. How I wished my mother could have joined us.

Budapest. 11. July. 1947.

KEREN KAJEMETH LEISRAEL

BUDAPEST, V, ARANY JÁNOS UTCA 29
TELEFON: 128-393

Uj cim: VII., Király-u 93. I.
Uj telefon: 225-856.

To whom it may concern.

This is to introduce Dr. Georg FRIEDLÄNDER, who as an old friend of the zionist movement rent several important services, especially respecting Displaced Persons and has been in strict terms with the Esra committee and other altruist organisations.

We beg all the concerning organisations and individuals to be at his particular help in all cases where necessity should arise and expedite his case.

Secretary,
K, K. L, Budapest, V., Arany János-u. 28.

Zionist letter of introduction

Registration certificate

George's Certificate

Onboard the SS Harry Taylor bound for America

Budapest after the war

Teenage years

The Italian Riviera, 1949

Weekend on the Danube

Ice Skating in Budapest

Our Apartment in Budapest

Celebrating the birth of Israel in Rome, 1948

Bologna, 1948

Rome, 1948

On the Spanish Steps in Rome

At the zoo in Rome

Rome, 1948

Rome Zoo

Shooting gallery in Rome

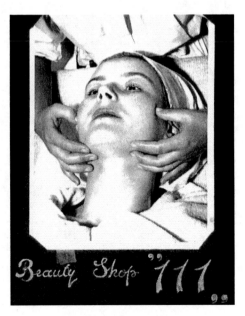

Beauty Institute in Rome

Italian Riviera, 1949

Trip to New York

Sunning in our backyard

Art lecture

With two admirers

With friends in Rome

Australia on business

Hawaii on business

Gift trade show

Rare snowstorm in Atlanta

Lynne with her horse, "Meathead"

Lewis, age ten

With Edit

Eva and Lewis

Dr. and Mrs. George Friedlander hold a 17th century painting by Sebastiano Ricci. The painting is titled simply, "'

At gallery opening

At gallery opening

ch 13, 1969

READYING FOR CONCERT — Members of the scenery comm
Kalb Civic Ballet are getting the sets in order for the ann
presented this year at DeKalb College March 21 and 22. Kneelin
Bill Nunn. On the table is Lynn Snipes, and others, left to rig
Beale and Kathy Banks.

DeKalb DAR Presents Award To Friedlanders

Baron DeKalb Chapter, Daughters of the American Revolution, has awarded Americaniam medals to two distinguished naturalized citizens, Dr. and Mrs. George Friedlander, of Atlanta. Mrs. P. I. Dixon, past regent of the chapter, made the awards at the chapter meeting at the Biltmore Hotel.

The Friedlanders, natives of Hungary, came to the United States in 1950 and became naturalized citizens in the Atlanta Naturalization Court in 1956.

Dr. Friendlander obtained his formal education in Hungary, France, Switzerland and Italy, earning his doctor's degree in physical chemistry at the University of Bologne. He was engaged as a research scientist and international coordinator for the National Institute of Health in Italy, and was a member of the research team that won the Nobel Prize for the discovery of penicillin.

After working in research at Emory University Medical School for several years, Dr. Friedlander went into industrial research. He now owns his own chemical manufacturing company and is a national and international consultant in chemistry. His position has taken him to all parts of the world, and he has become a collector of fine art and masterpieces.

Mrs. Eva Dukes Friedlander studied at the Fine Arts Academy in Rome. She has pioneered in importing the paintings of contemporary European artists, as well as various forms of art from Africa and the Far East, and has worked toward making art available to the public. She works as an art consultant in the Atlanta area.

Through their two children, Lewis, age 12, and Lynne, age 10, both Dr. and Mrs. Friedlander have been active in other community affairs, including Girl Scouts, Y.M.C.A., and Indian Guides. Dr. Friedlander coaches three youth soccer teams.

The Americanism medal of the DAR is awarded to adult naturalized citizens who have made outstanding contributions to our American way of life.

Eva Friedlander, Husband Receive D.A.R. Award

Pinning the medal on her husband is Eva Friedlander, Connoisseur Gallery.

Eva Friedlander, Assistant Buyer, Connoisseur Gallery, and her husband, George Friedlander, have been awarded Americanism medals by the Baron DeKalb Chapter, Daughters of the American Revolution. The award was presented to these two distinguished naturalized citizens February 28.

The Friedlanders, natives of Hungary, came to the United States in 1950 and became naturalized citizens in the Atlanta Naturalization Court in 1956.

Dr. Friedlander holds a doctorate degree in physical chemistry from the University of Bologne. He was engaged as a research scientist and international coordinator for the National Institute of Health in Italy, and was a member of the research team that won the Nobel Prize for the discovery of Penicillin. He now owns his own chemical manufacturing company and is national and international consultant in chemistry.

Mrs. Eva Friedlander studied at the Fine Arts Academy in Rome. She has pioneered in importing the paintings of contemporary European artists, as well as various forms of art from Africa and the Far East, and has worked toward making art available to the public.

Dr. and Mrs. Friendlander, through their two children, are active in community affairs, including Girl Scouts, Y.M.C.A. and Indian Guides. Dr. Friedlander also coaches three youth soccer teams.

The Americanism medal of the D.A.R. is awarded to adult naturalized citizens who have made outstanding contributions to our American way of life.

ANSWERS TO "WHAT'S OUR POLICY?" — Page 2

1. a.   3. c.
2. c.   4. a.

With George at an art exhibition

Dancing at Lynne's wedding reception

Lewis and Judy

Edit, our dog Binghi, and George

Lynne and Jeremy

Granddaughters Katarina and Eva Marie

Lynne, Marc, Jeremy and Ella

Eva Friedlander - 2010

Chapter 11

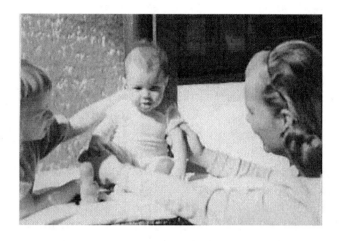

Another year passed before we could finally afford to send Mother a plane ticket to visit. It was so wonderful having her with me that I begged her to remain in America permanently, but she was adamant. "My life is in Budapest right now and yours is here with George and Lewis. I promise to come back soon."

No sooner had Mother returned to Budapest than George's mother, Hilda, arrived. By that time, I was pregnant again. "Didn't I predict that our first born would be a son?" he bragged. "This one will be a baby sister for Lewis."

I was nearing the end of my pregnancy, feeling like an elephant and in no mood to tolerate Hilda's high-handed attitude. She wasn't satisfied with anything — not the food I fixed or the way we were raising Lewis or even Atlanta with all the lovely azaleas and dogwoods in bloom. Because she made no attempt to learn English, it was impossible for her to make friends, or even converse with those who visited. Time was heavy on her hands. And mine. Her one saving grace was that she frequently prepared George's favorite fish soup — a delicious combination of carp, onions and garlic that could be eaten either warm or cold like aspic. She beamed with pride when we praised her cooking, but her pleasant mood seldom lasted through the evening.

On days she was particularly annoyed with me, she'd wait in the driveway for George to come home from work and present him with a litany of complaints about my housekeeping, our menagerie of animals, and imaginary ways that I had slighted her. Worst of all, she was a chain smoker, and despite the variety of ashtrays in every room, she rarely bothered to use one and I'd find a trail of ashes wherever she had been. Poor George. He tried to mediate between us, but more often than not, he was equally annoyed with her for not trying to fit into our household instead of expecting us to accommodate her every whim.

Mrs. Friedlander was pouting in her room puffing on a cigarette when George went in to tell her I had gone into labor. "Was she annoyed at having to stay home with Lewis?" I asked.

"She has no choice," he said. "We need someone to stay with him and she can't smoke on the maternity wing. I doubt she could last through your labor."

The next afternoon, I was still a little woozy after the birth of my perfect baby girl when my friend, Mildred, walked in to my hospital room where a small crowd had gathered to congratulate us.

"We stopped by the nursery to peek at the baby," she gushed. "Your daughter has her mother's lovely coloring and her father's gorgeous eyes. What did you name her?"

She looked from me to George who was sitting by my side with a cockeyed grin on his face. "Lynne Joyce Friedlander," we said almost in unison.

There was so much commotion in the room that it took me a few minutes to notice that Mildred had brought a stranger with her.

"I'd like for you to meet my friend, Sadie," she said. "Sadie, this is my dear friend, Eva."

I thought it odd that Mildred had brought a complete stranger to the hospital and even more bizarre that the woman wanted to come, but Mildred quickly explained.

"We're on our way to a luncheon," she said. "Wish you could come with us, but you have far more important things to do." The two women laughed, blew air kisses and slipped out the door.

"What a sexy lady that Sadie is," I said to George.

"Really, I didn't notice," he replied. Since he never missed a pretty woman whether he was at a party or the grocery store, I gave him a dirty look. But at that moment, I didn't care. I had just produced a beautiful little sister for our son.

"We really are a perfect American family," I murmured to George just before drifting into a happy sleep.

Back home, I stumbled through long days and sleepless nights and didn't think of Sadie again. Finally, after six months, George's mother finally left and my life went on. Being involved with the logistics of raising children, I was hardly aware of Sadie's assimilation into our group of couples until Marianne Baranan called.

"May I bring Sadie to your house on Saturday night?" she asked. "She just got a divorce and she's lonesome."

"Why not?" I said. "One more hamburger on the grill is no bother."

After that, Sadie became a regular at our house too. We found her witty, entertaining, and charming. She confided that although she was divorced, she and her husband still shared the same house.

"Isn't it a bit odd that Sadie and her husband live under the same roof even though they are divorced," I asked George as we tidied up after the party. "If it were me, I would never live in the house with my former husband."

He shrugged. "She's a very successful realtor, but I don't think his business is going well. The arrangement is likely financial." It was certainly none of my business and it never occurred to me that she and George were becoming an item.

The more I got to know Sadie, the better I liked her. With her too-tight clothing and wiggly hips, she added a certain joie de vivre to every party, and always the super saleswoman, she gravitated toward the men's group and chatted up real estate opportunities. They ate it up. Though she flirted openly with all the husbands, it seemed harmless enough and she endeared herself to the wives with her willingness to help clear the table or dry dishes.

As time went on, I couldn't help but notice how Sadie homed in on George like an aphid to a rose bush. I assumed it was because he was an up-and-coming chemist in Atlanta's booming chemical industry and she smelled opportunity. She adeptly divided him from the crowd and tempted him with photos of residential real estate opportunities. "This one is in a high growth area," she'd tell him. "That one is a fixer upper on the south side near the airport, but only needs cosmetic surgery. You can turn a profit quickly."

I didn't question her motive and even encouraged George to explore investment opportunities with her because in my mind, I could still hear my grandfather preach to my father. "Invest in real estate instead of your wild business schemes," he always advised. "The return may be slower, but in the end, the rewards will be far greater." Since failed business ventures proved my father's downfall, I couldn't help but think we should get involved in the same solid investments my grandfather touted.

"Let's invest a little money and see if we can turn a profit," I suggested to George. "A small risk would be worth it if it would help us put our children through college down the road."

So with my blessing, the two frequently met after work to drive around town looking at properties. Afterward, Sadie came back to the house to tell me what they had seen. I looked forward to these evenings and even prepared hors d'oeuvres or dessert and the three of us would share a drink and talk into the night. As time passed, their house hunting expeditions escalated and I was left out of the loop, but I held my tongue, convinced that real estate investments would be of great value to our family.

Months after they began their search, George and Sadie burst through the door. "I signed a contract today on our first property," he told me excitedly. "It's a single family home in a decent neighborhood and needs only fresh paint and a few minor repairs."

"You'll be surprised how quickly this one will sell," Sadie told me confidently.

George headed toward the liquor cabinet. "Let's celebrate," he said. "Do we have any snacks?"

Sadie was right. In short order, we turned a tidy profit and George invested in yet another property. Because he was so busy helping develop new industrial chemicals at Momar, she oversaw the renovations and advised us when the time was ripe to sell.

After the initial successes, I accepted Sadie as an integral part of our family life, still oblivious to the sexual tension between them. I thought it was strange that she stopped by the house so frequently in the late afternoon saying she was "in the neighborhood showing homes," but I attributed it to being lonely after her husband finally moved into his own apartment. Normally, she rang the door bell just as I was preparing dinner and it seemed rude not to invite her to join us.

Stupidly, I played right into their hands. Sadie was peppy and intelligent, a diversion for me from wiping drippy noses and toilet training. I enjoyed her witty chatter about transactions with the movers and shakers of Atlanta, and she entertained the children while I put the finishing touches on our dinner. Thread by thread, she wove her way into the fabric of our lives. She became someone I trusted.

Our mutual friends were equally smitten. Sadie's lifestyle was a tad Bohemian and between the real estate dealings that allowed her total control over her schedule and a grown son away at college, she had the freedom we stay-at-home moms envied. At the drop of a hat, she took off for North Georgia to see the trees in all their fall glory or hopped a plane to New York for a weekend of Broadway shows.

George coveted her carefree lifestyle. Though he tried to fit into suburbia, he, too, was a Bohemian at heart who longed to fly to New York on a whim or pile everyone in the car for some sun and fun in Miami. At the time, I thought their relationship was harmless. After all, he came home every night to the children and me and left Sadie to fend for herself.

My naïveté fed their fire.

Chapter 12

Five-year-old Lynne Friedlander holds Campi's painting.

Life zipped along at warp speed. The kids were growing like beautiful wild flowers and George received a handsome raise for developing a new water treatment chemical, Momar's most effective to date. All seemed to be going well until I received a call from New York that turned my life upside down.

"Is there someone at this number named Eva?" the voice asked.

"Yes, this is Eva. Who am I speaking to?"

"Do you know a woman named Edit Vadasz?"

"Of course I know her. She's my closest friend. What's the matter?" My heart began to race. "Is she all right?"

"I'm a nurse at Bellevue Hospital and a hotel clerk found your name and number on Ms. Vadasz' nightstand. She is recovering nicely now, but she tried to take her own life. We can't release her from the psychiatric unit without a responsible party. Can you come to New York and check her out?"

I was dumbfounded. I knew Edit had gone to New York to soothe her wounded heart after a painful breakup with her Caracas lover, but I had no idea she was despondent enough to try to take her own life.

I was panic-stricken. I had no one to leave the children with and they were too young to go with me. How could I drop everything and dash to New York? How could I not?

"I'll work things out and call you back in a few hours," I told her.

Frantically, I called George. "Calm down," he told me. "I'll see if I can take a few vacation days and fly up to bring her back here."

Apparently, he was just the tonic she needed. After three days of rest and recuperation, they flew to Atlanta. Unlike Mrs. Friedlander, Edit was an ideal houseguest and the children loved her. She was also a big help to me in launching my new antique business, funded with five-thousand dollars I received through the 1965 Federal Restitution Law to compensate people persecuted during the Holocaust. George was far from pleased that I invested my share in European art and antiques I planned to sell from home.

"How can you possibly make any money?" he complained. "You know nothing about running a business."

"Nothing?" I countered. "Have you forgotten that I ran my own secretarial business and helped you manage yours?"

Simple logic didn't phase him. I often heard him discussing what he called my "silly venture" with friends. But it wasn't until he began grousing to Edit that I understood what his gripes were really about.

As they shared coffee one morning while I prepared school lunches, I overheard Edit say, "Wasn't it a wonderful idea for Eva to launch her own business? I know you must be proud of her."

George apparently thought I was out of earshot. He retorted angrily, "She's not a leader, she's a follower. Her only skills are secretarial. I've got the only head for business in this family."

Edit was appalled — and furious. "Eva's extremely capable," she told him. "She was working at a law firm to support her mother and herself while you were in high school chasing girls. Then she opened a business when Hungarian women didn't do that sort of thing. Have you forgotten that she helped *you* too? Eva is one of the most capable people I know. She can do whatever she sets her mind to do."

Getting no sympathy, George muttered under his breath and stormed out the door.

"He feels threatened by you and can't bear the thought of sharing the limelight with anyone, not even his wife," she told me. "You'd better be wary. He may look to other women to get the adulation he craves."

I gave her a "you must be crazy" look and continued fixing breakfast for the two of us.

During the three months Edit lived with us, news of my antique business spread through word of mouth and ads I took out in *The Atlanta Journal* and *The Atlanta Constitution*. Within a short time frame, I achieved a measure of success. In fact, I got so busy that after Edit returned to Venezuela, I hired a combination nanny and housekeeper to give me the freedom to fly to England on buying trips. I also imported new original Italian oils that were signed by talented students. The new paintings sold well, but they were done in assembly line fashion and after six months, I decided that I was headed in the wrong direction. I returned to my real passion, fine antique paintings and furnishings. Future buying trips not only turned up some incredible pieces, I broadened my knowledge and made wonderful friends who invited me to stay in their homes instead of a hotel.

As my profits grew, George changed his tune. When he ran across a cache of antique oils on a business trip to Venice he called me, excitedly. "Eva, wire me two-thousand dollars immediately so I can buy ten extraordinary paintings," he said. "They're worth at least one-million dollars."

I was taken aback. "How do you know?" I asked. "Are you sure?"

"Daniel was with me and you know what a fine collection he and his wife have amassed. We believe the dealer has no idea about their value and wants to sell the entire lot for a pittance. It's the opportunity of a lifetime."

The next morning after I put the children on the school bus, I hurried to the bank to wire the money to George. My mind swirled with ways to spend the enormous profit we would reap. New cars for George and me. A horse for Lynne. A sleek new bike for Lewis. Some money to send Mother.

My dreams evaporated the moment I opened the crates containing the paintings. George, on the other hand, was so elated he strutted around proud as a peacock. "Aren't they wonderful," he asked. "You must call Sotheby's and Christie's tomorrow and put them into a high-roller auction."

I tried to tread lightly and not squelch George's enthusiasm too much. "They are lovely, but none of them are signed or authenticated," I told him. "That reduces their value immediately. I'm afraid that even though they're worth far more than the two-thousand dollars we paid for them, they'll never command the kind of money you envisioned."

"You're dead wrong. Six are attributed to two very famous seventeenth century painters, Sebastiano and Marco Ricci, who are credited with starting the romantic period of art in Italy. The rest are attributed to the school of Alessandro Longhi. I had to get permission from the Academy of Fine Arts of Venice to purchase and export them," he fumed.

"I hope you're right and I'm wrong, but I think the lack of signatures will be a big issue."

Unfortunately, I was right. After Sotheby's and Christie's both turned them down flat, George accused, "They don't know what they're talking about. Contact some museums directly."

It took him weeks to recover from the disappointment, and to make matters worse, none of my regular customers were interested in buying them. As time went by, I feared we would take a two-thousand dollar hit.

Finally, our friend Hugh Cates, the public relations manager at BellSouth, tipped off a writer at *Atlanta Journal* who came out to the house to take pictures for a big spread in the Sunday magazine section. The centerpiece was a photo of an adorable six-year-old Lynne standing on a chair next to a particularly large, handsome painting. Despite our high hopes, the publicity netted the sale of only one painting to a dentist from Mableton. It wasn't until George died decades later that I was able to get a considerable return on the investment. Even then, it was far, far less than he envisioned.

Over the years, my business grew exponentially and so did Sadie's presence in our lives. With her bedroom eyes and flirtatious nature, she remained the center of every party. The men openly joked about Sadie's sexy moves on George, but when questioned by friends, I laughed it off. "Don't be ridiculous," I told Julie, one of the more conservative members of the group. "She flirts with all the husbands, including yours."

An ideal business opportunity fell into my lap when George connected with a Hungarian friend living in Kenya who had begun exporting exquisite hand-carved lamps and figurines from India, Ceylon, and Africa. When he came to the house for dinner, he brought me a delicately carved elephant. All my friends raved.

"I think I should import these figurines," I told George. "I can lease a show room at the Atlanta Gift Mart during the semi-annual shows and if they sell well, I'll hire a sales rep. I think corporations would like them for their major holiday gift-giving." To my surprise, George was uncharacteristically supportive.

The gamble paid off almost immediately when I landed a huge order from the Coca-Cola Company — two-hundred pairs of hand-carved coconut wood elephants made in India. Everything ticked along like clockwork. The order was processed quickly and the shipment arrived in plenty of time for the Christmas deadline.

Excited to get a peek, I raided George's toolbox and pried one of the wooden crates open with a crowbar. I carefully extracted one pair of elephants from their straw bedding. Both had visible cracks. Panic mounted as I unwrapped one after the other in the same condition. I tore into the next barrel, then the next. By the time I reached the last one, elephants were laying all over the den floor like dead bodies in a hay grave. There was not one undamaged pair.

I called George at the office, "Every one of these damn elephants is cracked," I screamed. "What can I do? It's too late to get another trans-Atlantic shipment in time for delivery. You have to come home."

He appeased me by coming immediately and found me still sitting on the floor among the ruins. He picked up one pair after another.

"You're right. It's a bloody disaster," he said. "Those bastards! They must not have seasoned the wood before they turned it over to the carvers. I think the change in humidity during the long journey from Bombay to Atlanta caused them to crack."

I extricated myself from the carnage and we sank into the sofa, ignoring the elephant graveyard. "If I present these cracked figurines to the Coca-Cola executives, they have every right to refuse to pay me," I lamented. "I'll take a blood bath, in addition to losing all credibility for future orders."

"Let's not panic yet," he said. "I have to go back to work, but I'll talk to a few colleagues."

George left me alone to clean up the mess before the children came home from school, but by the time he returned that evening, he had a plan. "Warren Weingrad told me about a new compound called Wood Dough that repairs wood like new," he says. "If it works, we may be able to salvage the order."

Before he went to the office the next morning, George stopped by our local hardware store and purchased a dozen tubes of Wood Dough, sand paper and stain and brought them back to me. "Follow the directions on the label and call to let me know how it works," he said.

I went to work immediately smearing the sticky paste over the cracks, then wiping off the excess with my fingers and setting them aside to dry. The job was so tedious that by the time the children climbed off the school bus, I had finished only a dozen pairs. That night, George looked at them. "You've done about the best anyone could do," he said, giving me a rare compliment. "Nothing to do now but wait it out."

In the morning, we were almost afraid to look. But true to the brand's hype, the Wood Dough worked. We were beyond elated. George pitched in to get the children ready for school and I began sanding those damn elephants smooth as a baby's bottom, then re-stained them. To my delight, they appeared good as new.

Feeling there was light at the end of the tunnel, I spread the elephants on every conceivable flat space in the family room. If we could pull off the transformation in the two weeks remaining before the promised delivery date, the Coca-Cola executives would be none the wiser, I would reap a handsome profit and my reputation as a businesswoman would remain in tact.

In desperation over the time crunch, I recruited a few friends to help, Sadie among them. To make the chore more appealing, we set up an assembly line and served drinks and hors d'oeuvres in the evening while we worked. One person glued while others sanded and stained the elephants that had dried overnight. Sadie was the most faithful of the group and often stayed late into the night working with George while I put the children to bed and then fell into an exhausted asleep.

Delivery day dawned sunny and clear and just before re-sealing the barrels, I admired our handiwork. The cracks were totally invisible and our sanding and staining process was flawless. Best of all, when I delivered them, Coca-Cola's vice president of marketing told me, "This year's gifts are our best ever and will help promote Coke's global reach. It's been a pleasure doing business with you, Mrs. Friedlander. Perhaps you can find other unique items for us to have on hand when foreign dignitaries visit our headquarters throughout the year."

To celebrate our coup, George and I threw a party for our volunteers. Sadie wore a Coca-Cola red dress and had all the men in the palm of her hand. Although she toyed outrageously with all of them, her relationship with George was somehow different that evening. Our friend, Aaron, said to his wife within my earshot, "If Eva keeps inviting Sadie, George is going to take her to bed, and if he doesn't, I'm liable to."

I felt prickles pop under my skin as I glanced over at George and Sadie. They were sitting side by side on the sofa, her arm suggestively resting on his thigh. Throughout the evening, she seemed to attach herself to him. If they were standing, she touched his sleeve. If they were sitting, she found a way to rest her hand on the back of his neck. I even caught them playing footsies under the table.

As soon as the guests left, I erupted. "Do you think I'm blind and didn't notice how you and Sadie flirted tonight? Everyone was making jokes about the two of you. How dare you carry on like that in our home?"

"You know what a flirt she is," he said, dismissing me. "She doesn't mean anything by it."

"And what about you? What do you mean by it?"

He didn't answer.

The next morning, I was still seething, but as usual, I put on a smile for the children and began the day, knowing that the argument had not been put to rest. In fact, it was the beginning of a pattern of fighting that simmered beneath the surface. Some days began with bickering and ended in a stalemate. Others erupted and stayed on a high pitch for days.

About a month later, Marianne called to invite us over for poker night. "I'm not a big card player, as you know, but I'll ask George if he wants to come." As I suspected, he was eager to go. I didn't really mind. I was content to stay home with the children and work on a marketing plan for my latest shipment of antiques. Foolishly, I didn't think to ask if Sadie had been invited.

The following morning, Marianne called. "You should have been there last night," she said, laughing. "The party got a little raunchy, but it was great fun. After a few rounds of drinks, Sadie suggested we play strip poker instead of for our usual nickel stakes. Before we knew it, she had stripped down to her panties and bra. I suspect she was losing on purpose to show off those glorious boobs. I stopped the game about ten o'clock when she asked George to help her unhook her bra. It was hilarious."

I was furious. "How could you let her go on like that?" I shrieked. What were you thinking?"

She stammered. "I don't know what you're so upset about. You know how she is, especially if George is around. It was all in good fun."

After I banged down the receiver, I tried to remember what time George had come home. It certainly hadn't been anywhere near ten o'clock. Lynne had been up working on her third grade science project and about ten thirty I had gone into her room to tell her, "Lights out. Your project will have to wait until tomorrow after school."

I had read for a while longer, then finally turned out the light about midnight. George was still not home, but I wasn't worried. They often played cards into the wee hours — one of the reasons I didn't like to go. Still, I thought it strange that he hadn't mentioned the strip poker incident before he left for work.

The episode festered in my mind all day and by the time he came home for dinner, my anger boiled over. I slipped into my native tongue, Hungarian, the language of our fights throughout the years. "When were you going to tell me about the stripping party at Marianne's?" I demanded.

He threw back his head and laughed. "It was a riot," he said. "You should have been there. Marianne called the game to a halt just before Sadie unhooked her bra. The woman has no inhibitions."

"From what I understand, Sadie asked *you* to help her unhook it. If Marianne hadn't called me, would you ever have told me? Or is this another one of your little omissions where Sadie is concerned? Marianne said the game ended at ten. Where were you until the wee hours of the morning?"

George's eyes narrowed, a sure sign that his anger was mounting. "I drove her home, of course," he hissed. "She was in no condition to get behind the wheel of her car."

"She lives five minutes from Marianne's. Where were you the rest of the time?" I demanded.

"She could hardly walk so I helped her into bed," he said. "I would hope one of the other husbands would do the same for you."

"Are you insinuating that I would strip in front of friends and get so drunk I couldn't drive home? Just how stupid do you think I am? Don't even try to deny again that you slept with her, you son of a bitch. You've embarrassed and humiliated me for the last time." Without waiting for a rebuttal, I stomped into the bedroom and slammed the door, oblivious of my children who couldn't avoid hearing us.

George threw open the door. "You silly woman. This was nothing of great significance. Marianne and Aaron were there the entire time. So were the others. You're just looking for an excuse to pick a fight. I can't help it if

Sadie is flirtatious and provocative. That's just the way it is."

I didn't dignify his excuse. Instead, I picked up the phone and called my prime confidant, Marta Pruce, a Viennese psychiatrist married to an American doctor. On previous occasions, she had tried to mediate arguments about Sadie, but in her words, George was unwilling to admit any wrongdoing — ever. His mantra was always, "Eva is paranoid because she's so competitive with me. She doesn't seem to understand that Sadie and I have a business connection that will improve our family's financial situation. We don't have a sexual relationship." After our sessions, things usually improved briefly, but he would quickly resume his practice of not coming home for dinner, which precipitated even more bickering.

"I'm thinking of leaving George," I told her on the phone the evening after the strip poker incident. "Can Lynne and I stay with you for a few days so I can think things through?"

"Of course," she answered. "It will give us a chance to talk. But first, sit down with Lewis. Tell him he's welcome to come too."

I knew what Lewis's decision would be. He was a typically self-absorbed kid, heavily involved in wrestling, soccer, and karate. When I told him Lynne and I were going to Marta's for a few days and asked if he wanted to join us, he shrugged. "I'd rather stay here with Dad," he said. "I have wrestling tomorrow night and Dad always takes me anyway."

Lynne's reaction was just the opposite. She always identified with me and frequently tried to comfort me after George and I argued. "Don't let Daddy upset you, Mommy. You and I should go live in a log cabin in the mountains where we can have two horses and lots of dogs and cats."

But what does a child know? Her dream of our living on a farm apart from George and Lewis wasn't grounded in reality. Like most little sisters, she had a love-hate relationship with her big brother whom George clearly favored. "Daddy won't even miss us," she said. "He never pays attention to me anyway and all he does is fight with you."

She was right. Although George loved his daughter dearly, he focused much of his attention on Lewis and seemed bent on his son excelling at everything, from schoolwork to sports. He had great hopes that Lewis would either become the medical doctor George always wanted to be or follow in his footsteps as a chemist.

"We'll talk about moving to the country later," I told Lynne. "Right now we need to pack. Let's pretend we're off on an adventure."

Almost by rote, I put dinner on the table and sat down, trying to maintain a semblance of normalcy for Lewis and Lynne. The only words that I remember spoken were, "please pass the salt" from George and "are there any more potatoes" from Lewis. Lynne nervously pushed her food around her plate and I was so upset I stared at my portion. When the meal finally ended, I pushed back my chair and told George, "You and Lewis can clean up the dishes tonight. Lynne and I are ready to leave."

He looked stunned that I was carrying through with my threat. "How long will you be gone?" he asked.

I gloated inwardly. For once, he was worried. "I'll call you," I told him coldly, parroting the phrase he often said to me.

"But who will get Lewis off to school and to all his activities," he stammered.

"I guess you two will have to figure it out," I said. With that, Lynne and I picked up our suitcases and walked out the door.

In those days, no one locked their cars, so we had no problem putting the suitcases in the back seat, but when I reached for my keys to start the engine, I realized I had forgotten my purse. "Wait here," I told Lynne. "I'll be right back."

I knew I had made a huge mistake the moment I walked back inside. George's shock had turned into anger and he came at me with fire in his eyes. Somehow, I managed to grab my purse, dash back to the car and lock the door before he reached it.

"Open the door," he screamed, shaking the handle. "You're not leaving me."

I revved the engine as a warning, then put the car in reverse and inched backward, thinking surely he would step away. Instead, he flung himself across the windshield. Lynne started crying hysterically and I suppose in an effort to force him off the hood, she reached over and turned on the windshield wipers. The swift motion caught George off guard and he slipped to the ground. At that moment, I gunned the engine and backed out of the driveway.

By the time we arrived at Marta's, I was thoroughly traumatized. Lynne, on the other hand, quickly tucked the incident away. "Being here really is like going on a vacation, isn't it, Mommy?" she giggled. "We're going to have so much fun. Can I sleep in the bed with you?"

Numbly, I nodded. What had I done? I had not only left my husband, I had deserted my son. I was terrified that George would take out his anger on Lewis.

Marta took charge immediately. "You can sleep in the guest room," she told us. "Why don't you go unpack while Lynne and I have chocolate milk and cookies before bedtime?" Lynne was delighted to be treated like an honored guest, but I was a basketful of insecurity. I had threatened to leave George on several previous occasions, but this was the first time I had acted on it. I felt nauseous.

After Lynne went to bed, Marta poured us each a glass of wine and we stayed up talking late into the night. "I can't live like this," I told her. "There are times when I hate George for what he is doing to me and our family. I've been on the fence until now, but this strip poker incident is the last straw. Sadie is after my husband and I'm almost ready to let her have him. "

"I understand your anger, but whatever your differences, you have to stop fighting in front of the children," she told me gently. "Lynne is much too knowledgeable about the situation for a nine-year-old. She tells me that she doesn't need an alarm clock in the morning because the sound of your arguing in Hungarian wakes her up."

I began to cry. "I know, I know, but I can't help myself. I always intend to wait until the children go to bed to confront him, but as soon as George walks in the door I lose my temper. Sometimes when he gets really angry, he squeezes my arms so tightly I have bruises that last for weeks. He says it's my fault because I provoke him. I suppose he's right. Why else would he look for someone else?"

Marta frowned and held up her the palm of her hand. "Stop right there. There is nothing you did to warrant his unfaithfulness and he has no right to hit you. Ever. Nor to grab you so hard he leaves bruises. Underneath that debonair exterior, he obviously has a vicious temper he must learn to control, regardless of who provokes whom. The two of you seem to have a total lack of communication. Do you ever talk any more without screaming at one another?"

Over the next few days, she and I talked at length about my options. Basically, it came down to two things. I could take the children and leave George or remain with him, but insist on intense counseling. "Think long and hard, too, about whether you still love him and if you think your marriage is worth saving," she said.

During the day while she was with clients and Lynne was at school, I examined my heart, which was truly broken. I had always felt we were a team. Hadn't I helped him set up his office in Budapest, partnered with him at the salon in Rome, and worked equally as hard when we arrived in America? Sex between us had always been good. How could he have betrayed me?

I weighed my choices carefully. Although divorce in the 1960s was not a scandal, the process was far more complicated than it is today. Nor was divorce as accepted. If I hinted at spousal abuse, would people believe me – the wronged wife — or the loud denials of a well-respected scientist? Whatever the outcome, the allegation alone would bring scandal to all of us.

Socially, it would also be a blow. Few women moved as easily in couple circles as Sadie and I hardly fit the picture of a gay divorcee. What's more, divorce was abhorrent to me. Even as an adult, the haunting memory of my father's desertion preyed heavily on my self-esteem and I didn't want that cloud to hang over my children.

Finances were also a huge consideration. My antique business was doing well, but I didn't make enough to support myself and the children without considerable help from George, and I wasn't sure I could count on him for much since there would be two households to fund. Dragging my children into the poverty I had experienced as a young girl positively terrified me. Where would we live? The deed to the house was solely in George's name and I felt certain he wouldn't leave willingly. Besides, in my heart of hearts, I still loved George and had signed the Ketuba, promising to remain "for better or worse."

After the war, people always joked that like a cat, George had nine lives. If I was the betting kind, I would guess that he had already used up more than one of the lives of our marriage, as well.

Chapter 13

On the fourth day after our departure, I dropped Lynne by school and returned home. That afternoon, Lewis threw himself at me. "Aw, Mom," he said. "I'm really glad you're home. I missed you."

His enthusiasm convinced me I had done the right thing and I prepared my husband's favorite meal, Chicken Paprika, a prelude to my insistence that we get more counseling. Like Lewis, he gave me a bear hug, relieved that Lynne and I had returned.

He even begrudgingly agreed to meet with Marta on a weekly basis. Sometimes we went together; other times individually. After months, we had still not reached a resolution, primarily because George continued to hold steadfast to the notion that he had done no wrong. He argued that I exaggerated the significance of the poker game and dismissed the incident of throwing his body on the hood of the car as a "joke." Exhausted with rehashing the same argument, I gave up.

Years later, I found a letter Marta had written to another psychiatrist referring George. "I found him to be unstable emotionally, flaring up easily and exhibiting a great deal of anxiety with restlessness and profuse perspiration," she wrote. She also felt he had difficulty with authoritative figures which created difficulty at work. Her assessment explained his erratic behavior and I couldn't help but wonder if he had ever seen the psychiatrist Marta recommended. Had I been privy to this information, would it have changed anything? I doubt it.

In addition to my devotion to my children, I also took comfort in our menagerie of animals, likely because I never had animals of my own growing up. George, too, welcomed all strays, including Rainy, a tiny gray tabby cat Lewis found mewing on the side of the road. Like George, he got into one scrape after another, but always seemed to land on his feet and even outlived his master.

Lynne loved the collection of dogs and cats and by the time we went to Marta's, she had been volunteering for more than a year at the local Humane Society where she helped feed and groom the dogs and cats. One day when I picked her up, she was bursting with news. "They found a poor, sick horse on the expressway and he's going to live in the shed behind the shelter," she said excitedly. "They said I could help feed him the next time I come. Can I go back tomorrow, Mommy, pu-lease?"

"Why not?" I answered. "Lewis has a soccer game and your father will be there with him."

Nearly every afternoon after the horse arrived, Lynne begged me to take her to the shelter. "I named him Meathead and he lets me pet his nose and groom and feed him," she said. "When he gets stronger, Mr. Bob says I can walk him around the barn and maybe even ride him."

Thanks in part to Lynne's loving care, Meathead regained his strength quickly. Instead of being devastated when he was put up for adoption, she was thrilled.

"Mommy, isn't it wonderful? Now we can adopt Meathead. I promise you won't have to do anything. I know how to feed and groom and exercise him. All we need is a place for him to live."

I put my arms around her. "Sweetie, it's not as easy as all that. Horses are very expensive. We'll have to talk to your father."

She burst into tears. "You know Daddy will never let me have Meathead. Lewis gets to do whatever he wants and I don't ever get to do anything."

I made up my mind at that instant. Lynne was going to have her horse, regardless of George's objections. As I look back, I think my motive was two-fold. I not only wanted to counteract George's devotion to Lewis, I was also courting Lynne's favor so I could keep her solidly in my camp should there ever be a permanent separation.

"Oh Mommy, thank you. You won't be sorry, I promise."

Meathead wound up living in her friend Wendy's, barn about five miles from our house. The arrangement worked well and the girls had a wonderful time riding together. Wendy also encouraged Lynne to enter Meathead in horse shows, and despite the added expense,

I beamed with pride when she began to excel. I never missed a single event. George, on the other hand, never once came to watch her compete.

The only bad experience Lynne and I had during the two years we owned Meathead had everything to do with the weather and very little to do with the horse. On an unseasonably warm February morning, I sent Lynne to school in only a lightweight jacket, but during the day, the temperatures plummeted. By the time I picked her up from school to feed Meathead, plump beautiful snow flakes had begun to fall, turning Atlanta into a winter wonderland.

We had no problem driving the five miles to the horse stall where we fed both horses quickly, then hurried back to the car, which I had parked on the edge of the huge Buckhead property. Lynne was shivering.

"Don't worry," I assured her. "As soon as the engine warms up, we'll be toasty." How I wish. When I tried to pull the car away from the curb, the wheels whirred in the snow, which had turned to ice. I tried over and over. "Baby, even if I can get the car out on the road, I don't think we can negotiate the icy hill. We have no other choice but to walk."

"It's a long, long way home, Mommy," Lynne whimpered. "I've never walked that far before."

"I haven't walked five miles in a long, long time, but we'll make it. Nothing can stop the Friedlander girls, right?"

A perusal of the trunk yielded no stray jackets or blankets, so we zipped up our thin jackets and plunged our hands in our pockets, hoping to find a pair of gloves. Between us, we came up with one. I grabbed Lynne's right hand and put it in my left pocket and we alternated hands and the glove as we plodded home. Four endless hours later, we finally reached our house, frozen, soaked to the bone, and exhausted.

"Where in the world have you been?" George asked, flinging open the door and gathering both of us to him. "I've been worried sick. The soccer game was called due to the weather and I couldn't imagine what was taking you so long. Get into a warm shower immediately or you'll both catch pneumonia."

Without taking time for an explanation, we gratefully complied, thankful to be safely home. Steaming hot baths, dry clothes, and hot chocolate warmed us inside and out. Only then did George ask, "Why did you and Lynne walk? What's happened to the car?" For once, he listened intently without interruption and pulled Lynne up on his lap.

Chapter 14

During the first dozen years of our marriage, George was a staunch Democrat and backed several candidates in the 1964 election. His favorite was Charles Weltner, a prince of a fellow who was running for Congress. "He's the polar opposite of our former Hungarian friends and neighbors who turned their backs on Jews during the Nazi era," George said. "Charles took a tough stand when he openly supported the 1954 Supreme Court ruling outlawing segregation in the public schools and I want to see him elected."

Charles's success in the election didn't dampen his enthusiasm for taking on the southern establishment during the Civil Rights era, one of the most tumultuous times in this country's history. In 1964, he cast an affirmative vote for Lyndon Johnson's Civil Rights Act and then backed the Voting Rights Act — both highly unpopular moves.

Over lunch one day after his election, Charles said, "I'm so grateful for the support you and Eva gave me, especially the gathering with all of your neighbors. Is there anything I can do for you?"

George thought it over a few minutes, then joked, "Get Eva and me tickets for Lyndon Johnson's inauguration." A few weeks later, a fancy gilded envelope containing an ornate invitation to the inauguration and ball arrived in the mail. We were surprised, to say the least.

"What in the world am I going to wear?" I asked.

George didn't hesitate. "I want to go with you to select a gown," he said. "My wife must be the most beautiful one at the inauguration."

For the first time in our lives, we didn't worry about the expense. My final selection was a long, sleek deep blue number covered in sequins with a sexy slit to the knee. I bought matching shoes and bag and rented a long, elegant black velvet coat. George, of course, purchased an Armani tuxedo.

We talked of nothing else leading up to our departure, excited to have secured a room at the Hay Adams near the White House. The inauguration itself took place on January 20, 1965, and the ball that evening was magical. We were surrounded by luminaries like the suave film star Cary Grant and witty Dorothy Kilgallen and Arlene Frances from the popular television show, "What's My Line." As usual, George worked the crowd expertly and we mingled with politicians, governors, and executives whom he charmed with his extensive knowledge of science and international politics, as well as history and architecture. I was very proud to be on his arm that evening.

Unfortunately, things did not bode as well for Charles's political future. Although he had endeared himself to President Johnson with his affirmative Civil Rights votes, he angered Georgia's Democratic Party leaders. When his term in Congress came to a close in 1968, the party demanded that he sign an affidavit of loyalty to arch segregationist Lester Maddox, who was running for governor. Charles refused and, knowing he couldn't be reelected to Congress without the party's financial support, he decided not to run for a second term. A few years later, he lost his bid for mayor of Atlanta to Maynard Jackson.

The euphoria of our trip to Washington sustained us for a time and on the surface, we lived a full life — entertaining clients and friends, dealing with the children's issues, sometimes struggling financially. In reality, life was far better than we dared dream about while fearing for our lives during the Nazi era, then again during Russia's stronghold over Hungary.

Despite the specter of Sadie's shadow, we had many memorable moments like the time we took the children to Chastain Park so George could give Lewis a few tips on passing and heading a soccer ball. "That man walking toward us looks familiar," I whispered. "I think it's Martin Luther King and that must be one of his sons."

George cocked his head in disbelief, but as we drew closer, he concurred. "I'm going to go say hello. You and Lewis hurry along." As we converged on the famous Civil Rights leader, others recognized him too. All we managed was a brief exchange about George's keen interest in popularizing soccer in America and bringing a professional soccer team to Atlanta. Within a few moments, Dr. King was surrounded by a crowd of admirers and we faded into the background.

Just a few years later, we were heartbroken when we heard the news that Reverend King had been shot and killed. George fell into a depression that lasted long after the rest of the country returned to a semblance of normalcy.

Regardless of harboring considerable bitterness over his continuing affair with Sadie, I still felt the pull of my husband's power to cast a spell over me. Out of the blue he would bring me huge flower arrangements or suggest we go out for a gourmet dinner. I suspected it was mostly an act, but he had the uncanny ability to theoretically hold my hand and Sadie's at the same time.

Just as he could act the model husband, he could turn on a dime, picking fights about anything and everything and then using the current argument as an excuse to absent himself from dinner. His justification was always the same. "I have a business meeting and we'll grab a bite to eat before I come home," or "I have to catch up on some paperwork." If I pressed him for details, his answer was deliberately vague. Sometimes he gave no indication that he wouldn't be home and I'd feed the children and oversee their homework, then eat a cold dinner alone. And seethe.

When George finally came in, he'd tiptoe into the bedroom and whisper loudly, "Are you asleep?" I would deliberately mumble something unintelligible.

Then he'd say "What is there to eat?"

One night I shot straight up in the bed. "I thought you were having dinner with a client," I accused. "Why would you be hungry?"

"We wound up just getting drinks," he whined. "I'm starving."

"You expect me to believe that you just had drinks? Sadie must be pretty good in bed to make you forget to eat dinner."

George stomped out of our bedroom and I could hear him rattling around in the refrigerator looking for leftovers. For months at a time, I could barely look at him, much less sleep with him. The thought of him going from her bed to mine was disgusting. I knew I was perpetuating an already terrible situation, but I didn't have the desire to change it.

Chapter 15

She lectures on art collecting

, Ha Friedlander, a North Side art lecturer on art and antiques, works of art by contemporary European artists in her small gallery in her home. She also travels to Europe about once each year to collect contemporary and traditional paintings to show and for her personal collection. (Photo by Vivian Price).

Nine years after George joined Momar, he left to accept a position at Zep Manufacturing Co., a well-established industrial chemical firm, where he was hired to bring in international customers. He traveled incessantly, talking with trade commissions in far-flung places from Australia, New Zealand and Hawaii to Colombia. Since he was the only employee in that capacity, Zep had given him carte blanche to write his own agenda, but after several years, they came to the conclusion that George's accomplishments didn't match his considerable travel expenses.

He immediately put out feelers with contacts he had established while working at Zep, and accepted a position as technical director at a pool chemical company. I assumed his travel would subside so he could spend more time at home, but it wasn't long before he began spending two or three evenings a week out, which he blamed on his stressful new job.

It wasn't a partnership made in heaven and the relationship between George and the owner quickly evolved into a power struggle.

We argued about it constantly. "It's never a good business idea to bring a mistake your boss has made to his attention," I warned. "One day, he will reach the end of his rope and fire you."

"He'll never do that," George said. "I'm the only one around there with the brains to develop new products." I sighed. My husband had never liked answering to anyone — particularly a boss — but his brilliance had usually trumped his insubordination and I had faith it would again.

As the weeks passed, George's preoccupation with work escalated and he spent more and more evenings away from home. He kept telling me that a new "formula" wasn't living up to expectation, but I was highly suspicious that his "formula" was named "Sadie." I never dreamed that his job was in jeopardy.

After what must have been a particularly rancorous morning, he called at lunchtime. "I'm on my way home," he said, his voice flat. "Roger and I will never get along. I've parted ways with the company."

During the interminable wait for him to pull into the driveway, I vacillated between anger and terror. We had a hefty mortgage, two growing children, and unpaid bills. Plus, I sent money to Mother every month. How were we going to manage?

When George walked in with a cardboard box filled with his office supplies and plopped down on the couch a defeated man, my anger dissipated. Without a word, I walked over to the liquor cabinet and poured him half a glass of vermouth with a twist of lemon — his favorite.

He took a few gulps, then began talking.

"You'll have to find a full-time job until I can find a new position," he told me. "If Roger blackballs me in the industry, it could take some time." After his putdowns through the years about my capabilities in the business world, the irony of George admitting *I* could find a job more easily than he could was delicious. This could be my golden opportunity to plunge into the antique world on a much grander scale.

At the same time, the idea of going to work full time was daunting. I quickly made a mental list. I needed to make sure our wonderful housekeeper, Lola, was willing to be flexible with her schedule, buy a new business wardrobe, and most important, find a position with an income that would potentially replace George's.

It was far easier than I imagined. By sheer accident, I heard of an opening in the Connoisseur Gallery (antique department) at Rich's, the city's finest department store whose name was synonymous with quality and service. I was obviously in the right place at the right time because I was hired on the spot by the buyer, Lila Campbell, who had been hand picked by Dick Rich, the store's founder.

She took an immediate shine to me, and I to her. We had much in common. Both of us had been encouraged as children to study the arts and had pursued our studies into adulthood. While she audited classes at the University of Georgia, I had attended fine arts courses at the Accademia di Belle Arte during our time in Rome.

"With our combined knowledge of European art, we'll turn this department into one that rivals any fine New York shop," she said. Her words sent my self-esteem soaring.

The job of assistant buyer at Rich's proved the perfect salvo to our finances and my satisfaction with life. Soon after my arrival, Lila confessed that her health was failing and that she wanted to groom me to take over her job. I took my new responsibilities very seriously, frequently staying late to work with her.

I also made it a point to be among the first to arrive. Nearly every morning, Mr. Rich and I would ride the elevator together. He was interested in every aspect of the department and always inquired about our new acquisitions or ask my opinion on new initiatives. Known throughout the South as a brilliant merchandiser who believed that the customer was always right, he expected clerks to keep records of our client's preferences and call when something they might like came in. He also had a "no-questions asked" policy on returns and all the department heads joked about the items with labels from other stores that we accepted, but couldn't re-sell. Mr. Rich didn't care about this small loss of revenue. He knew that the policy would build a cadre of loyal customers who refused to shop anywhere else. He was right.

As head of the antique department, I worked hand-in-hand with other managers who took pride in using our merchandise to enhance their displays. Handsome pieces artfully arranged amid clothing, jewelry, even gardening items added the flavor and elegance Mr. Rich wanted throughout the store.

Shortly after my arrival, Dan Carithers, the highly talented head of design came up with the idea of turning the store into an Italian piazza for a special event focusing on merchandise imported from my former temporary country. Mr. Rich loved the idea and gave Dan carte blanche to purchase full-size gondolas, red and white striped mooring poles, fabulous wrought iron gates, and statues that transformed the city department store into a little Italian village. Every department head went into high gear seeking out unique Italian merchandise to feature. We augmented the displays with Renaissance chairs and fine antique tapestries to show off the Italian items. The famous Magnolia Room featured Italian dishes and breads and singing gondoliers entertained throughout the day. The extravaganza was a huge success and we were proud of our part in it.

Even though I had traveled to England on buying trips many times on my own, Lila opened new doors on our first buying trip to Chelsea and London. She was a master in ferreting out the best buys from local dealers and bidding on items at auctions. At Sotheby's and Christie's, she introduced me to famous artists and renowned antique dealers. I retained these initial contacts throughout my career and built on them as time passed. These buying trips were a tonic and I always came home buoyed by my experiences and the opportunity to broaden my knowledge. They also allowed me to slip away from my pervasive marital problems.

George's anger over his inability to find another position he deemed "suitable" exacerbated our situation at home. He refused to give me any credit for landing such a prestigious job or even for my quick promotion to buyer when Lila left three months later.

"Her buying trips to Europe give Eva an opportunity to go spend Mr. Rich's money while I'm stuck at home searching for the right opportunity," he told our friends. In public, I tried to laugh his hurtful comments off. At home, it was a different story.

My job not only brought me huge personal satisfaction, it had some wonderful unexpected consequences. To get the word out about our expanding antique department, Rich's submitted my name to the Atlanta Speakers Bureau and I was invited to make frequent presentations to large women's groups. Our friend Hugh Cates once again came to my aid by asking me to speak to many of the large convention groups BellSouth hosted. Sometimes I talked about antiques, art, and Persian rugs, but primarily my speeches were about my passion for America and gratitude for living in a free country.

Although I settled into my new position with ease, George had a far more difficult time being unemployed – a blow to his ego and to his dreams to make a splash in the business world. Three months went by without a glimmer of a job. And each evening I had to steel myself to face his dark moods. One evening, he surprised me by being unusually buoyant. When I spotted a lovely bouquet of pink and red roses in the center of the dining room table and drinks set out on a silver tray, I assumed he had landed a job.

"There's something I want to talk with you about," he said, so excited his words seemed to tumble on top of one another. "I've been developing some new industrial cleaning formulas that aren't yet on the market. What would you think about my going into business for myself? I've located an abandoned building on Ashby Street that has storage tanks, plumbing and the necessary infrastructure built in. Since it's been empty for a while and is in pretty deplorable shape, the rent is cheap and the owner says I can take possession in thirty days." He paused and looked at me expectantly like a little boy waiting for permission to dive into a box of Oreo cookies.

I didn't hesitate. "It's a wonderful idea," I told him. "You'll never be content under someone else's thumb and we'll reap the profits instead of your bosses." George was so elated over my response, he gave me a bear hug, something he hadn't done for months. I saw a glimmer of hope that if the business kept him busy enough, he wouldn't have time for Sadie and we might mend our marriage.

Things moved along quickly. George secured a small business loan and I rolled up my sleeves to help clean and paint the interior. I also interviewed and recruited personnel, including our yardman, Clyde, who, despite a lack of any formal education and an inability to read and write, was an eager learner. Besides, he had common sense to spare and was extremely trustworthy.

"How would you like to work for my husband at his new business, Custom Chemicals?" I asked as he was trimming bushes.

"Miz Friedlander, I don't know nothin' about chemicals. Do you want me to do yard work at the doctor's office?"

"No, Clyde. My husband wants you to learn to mix chemicals and handle the shipping and receiving."

Clyde took off his baseball cap and scratched his head. As soon as I mentioned the salary -- double what he could make doing lawn work — he asked, "Can I start tomorrow?"

We had not misjudged him. Using a color-coding system he and George devised, Clyde quickly learned the ropes. In his twenty-five years with Custom Chemicals, he never failed to fulfill an order accurately.

As for George, he was not only more content than he had ever been, he proved to be very talented, not only developing new formulations, but in luring customers away from rival suppliers. His specialty was cleaning products customized to meet the needs of the various industries the company served like Delta Airlines, Dalton Carpets, and poultry processing plants. Business was so brisk he was soon able to hire outside salesmen and a secretary, freeing me from typing invoices after the children went to bed.

This period of our lives should have been very exciting. George had his own business, I had found my own niche as manager of the antique department at a major department store and the children were thriving. But instead of treating me like an equal partner, George remained fiercely competitive, always emphasizing his own importance and telling me in no uncertain words that my accomplishments paled in comparison to his. And much to my dismay, Sadie hovered in the background. I had no doubt that she wanted to become wife number two.

In public, George used me as a front to round out his business persona. He took me on business trips and we hosted dinner parties in our home for his customers. Even when I felt the evening had gone particularly well and the guests had cleaned their plates, he found something to criticize, whether it was the quality of the food or the appearance of the table. He never failed to snatch defeat from the jaws of victory.

One evening after a pleasant gathering, he confronted me in the kitchen. "The Chicken Paprika was not up to par this evening. What did you do differently?" he complained. "Why in the world did you choose the green table cloth instead of that elegant white one I brought you from Belgium?" In his eyes, I could do no right.

At Rich's, it was just the opposite. Mr. Rich constantly praised my efforts and four years after I began, he chose me as the first antique buyer at the new Lenox Mall store in the posh Buckhead area. I was thrilled over the opportunity to open the department and promised him that we would equal or exceed sales at the downtown store. I was true to my word and a year later, both departments were drawing in so much revenue that Mr. Rich hired an English antique dealer to oversee the combined antique, furnishings, decorative arts, and flooring departments at both stores.

I admit that I was disappointed that he hadn't approached me for the position, but that did not color my reaction to the new Englishman. From the onset, we didn't get along — nor did he get along well with other department heads. Although he was capable and talented, he lacked the warmth and charm of English people in the antique business I had met through the years. Instead of trying to build an esprit de corps, he found constant fault. A little dust on a handsome Louis XIV table was blown up to the level of a major catastrophe that we heard about for days, and if a customer walked away without making a purchase, he demanded to know why.

"He wants to build himself up at the expense of the rest of us," a colleague grumbled. I didn't say it out loud, but his attitude mirrored George's.

Because he was at the downtown store and we had little contact, I hung on for nearly a year, but gradually, I became disenchanted with his interference. An opportunity dropped in my lap when I met Jane Threlkeld and Dorothy Schlemon, owners of Threlkeld-Schlemon, Assoc., Ltd., a well-established antique showroom at the Atlanta Decorative Arts Center (ADAC). The timing was perfect. They were looking for an art expert and I was in need of a new challenge. To bring even more value to the business, I took a course to become a Certified Art Appraiser, a skill that has brought me great pleasure and extra income through the years.

Shortly after I joined Jane and Dorothy, two handsome young Iranian men walked into the showroom hoping to find a partnership to market the Persian rugs they imported from Iran, Turkey, and China. I was excited over the prospect. The addition of fine rugs would set our business apart and give designers yet another reason to choose us over the myriad of others featuring antiques. Though neither Jane nor Dorothy had extensive knowledge of rugs, I had grown up with parents and grandparents who collected rugs and had learned to distinguish among the different styles. I learned far more when we lived in Rome and I've never forgotten the mantra of my favorite Italian instructor: "Good design begins with the floor."

Once again, the timing was right. During the 1970s, wealthy homeowners had a keen interest in owning fifty- to seventy-five-year-old antique carpets that were sought for both their beauty and their investment value. Designers were equally intrigued with promoting carpets ranging in price from ten-thousand to sixty-thousand dollars because the higher the cost, the greater their commission.

Jane, Dorothy, and I put our heads together and decided to dedicate an entire department to showcase the various carpets named for the cities or tribal regions where they were hand woven. Serapis, Kashan, and Heriz plus rugs woven by primitive tribes were all extremely popular, each remarkable for its coloration, pattern and weave.

American homeowners accustomed to factory perfection had a hard time grasping the concept that the more uneven the pattern and the more deviations in a carpet, the more valuable. These irregularities were indications that the yarns had been hand-dyed and hand woven from memory rather than manufactured, which only added to a rug's mystique and value.

As our reputation grew, so did the percentage of our business from the sale of these fine carpets. I became known as the go-to expert and designers frequently asked me to accompany them to clients' homes to help them choose the perfect rug for the space. Occasionally, two or three trips were necessary, but we were more than willing because satisfied customers were our best advertisement.

To further promote our business and increase my visibility as an expert, I lectured to students and designers at the Art Institute of Atlanta, the Atlanta International School, and at large gatherings. I was cited repeatedly in *Architectural Digest* for being an expert in the field. Twice a year, our showroom hosted two-day seminars where I demonstrated the different rug styles. I stayed abreast of the field by continuing my studies.

Much to my surprise, I was asked to "ghost" design for a major designer who had been hired to redecorate all the state judges' private offices. We worked together selecting eighteenth century furnishings, accessories, and draperies that were sufficiently dignified for their position without appearing ostentatious.

The project was so well received, the designer invited me to collaborate on even larger projects. We spent hours poring over blueprints to plan furniture placement and choose color schemes, furnishings, fabrics, accessories, art and carpets from ADAC showrooms. To further my knowledge, I took additional classes at the Art Institute in drafting, reading blue prints, and lighting, which further added to my self-confidence.

An unexpected partnership fell into my lap when a designer who specialized in funeral homes and mausoleums asked me to assist her. Instead of using somber colors and dark wood paneling, we brightened the spaces with pastel colors, pastoral scenes, and florals. Funeral directors loved the color palette since it helped alleviate the depression inherent in their somber profession.

Despite this hectic schedule I agreed to yet another challenge when my partners suggested I enter a contest to design a live/work space studio apartment for a designer. For weeks, I slaved over the elevations, floor plan, and drawings and though I was pleased with my efforts, I had no notion that I would win anything at the twice-yearly two-day conference hosted by ADAC. When my name was called as the first-place winner, George jumped up from his chair and gave me a giant hug, then stuck by my side all evening, brimming with pride.

The evening was but a small oasis in our marital desert because little improved at home. The more independent and successful I became, the more I resented George's vehement denials that he and Sadie were having an affair. His refusal to give me access to our financial information and include my name on the deed to the house only added to my discontent and became a prime source for future arguments. Whether he acknowledged it or not, I was an equal partner in the marriage, contributing to our family on all levels, domestic and professional. Why were my contributions not enough? Why did he need Sadie?

Admittedly, there were many times I was a shrew, matching his verbal barbs with aplomb. My frequent, often daily, outbursts only made things worse and the distance between us swelled from a puddle to a chasm as broad as the Danube. I widened the gap further by withholding intimacy. But who could blame me? After a long day at work, cleaning up after dinner and helping the children with their homework, I was in no mood for intimacy with a man who was cheating on me.

On the occasional evening he did come home, the phone always rang during our rare dinners as a family. If I answered, there was an audible click. Magically, if George answered, there was always a real person on the other end. From his reaction, I could tell it was Sadie. He would leave his food on the table, put his hand over the mouthpiece and tell us, "This is an important business call." Then he'd drag the long telephone cord into his study.

I could feel my blood pressure rise. Even though the door was closed, his voice carried. He complained about the way I nagged him and how *she* was the only one who appreciated him. Sometimes, he discussed personal family matters. Later, when I confronted him, he was defensive.

"What right do you have to listen through the closed door? Besides, you have it all wrong. She was asking my advice on a personal matter."

For self-protection, I absented myself emotionally. The atmosphere in our home had all the warmth of a refrigerator, and our marital bed was a block of ice. I would have preferred being on a different continent.

Lynne remembers those years clearly and constantly begged me to leave him. "I don't understand why you don't divorce Dad," she said repeatedly. "He doesn't care about you and me anyway — only about Lewis. I don't even want to have a birthday party this year because he'll make a scene and storm out like he always does and spoil it. He can't stand it if he's not the center of attention all the time."

I couldn't deny her observation. For a preteen, she had incredible insight to an adult situation. While I was growing and developing my business, learning more and stretching my creativity, George tried to tear down everything I accomplished. If he couldn't be the focus of female adoration in his family, he would find it elsewhere, regardless of our marriage vows and the work we had done in counseling.

Sadie, of course, was able to maintain her total devotion to George. She didn't have to take over as the wage-earner in our family, only to be belittled. She didn't have to mediate between a child who legitimately wanted some attention from her father and a self-absorbed man who was more concerned with his self importance than with his daughter's interests.

At this point of our undeclared war for his love and admiration, I had to concede that Sadie was winning.

Chapter 16

Despite all the acrimony at home, we were the epitome of a happily married couple to the outside world. We were in the midst of a business dinner with George's clients at a wonderful Italian restaurant, La Grotta, when I received an emergency message from our baby sitter. "You'd better come home, Mrs. Friedlander," she said. "A Hungarian doctor called that your mother is critically ill."

I was stunned. In our last conversation, Mother hadn't mentioned anything about being sick. Could she have had a heart attack?

We excused ourselves quickly and dashed home so I could return the call. Finally, after several agonizing tries, Dr. Kovacs came to the phone. "Your mother took an overdose of sleeping pills and tried to commit suicide," he told me. "Luckily, a neighbor found her. She's stable for the time being, but her condition is still precarious. Can you come to Hungary? She keeps asking for you."

"I'll be there as soon as I can arrange things here," I assured him. "Please tell her I'm on my way."

George was uncommonly supportive. "Go pack," he said. "I'll arrange for your plane ticket, but there's likely no rush. We probably can't get you out of Atlanta until tomorrow morning. Go to bed now and try to get a good night's sleep. You're not to worry about me or the children, we'll be fine."

Needless to say, I was sick with worry and barely slept that night. Every time I closed my eyes, I imagined the worst. The eight-hour plane ride was no better. I felt like yelling at the pilot, "Can't you go any faster?"

The minute I landed, I hailed a taxi for the hospital. As the familiar sights of beautiful Budapest swept past the window, I found that despite the circumstances, I was happy to be in my homeland again. Pleasant memories of the good times — school days, boyfriends, falling in love with Dan — flooded over me and the terrible war years faded in the distance. I prayed my trip wouldn't end in tragedy.

To my great relief, Mother was awake and responsive. "What haven't you been telling me?" I cried, falling into her arms. "Why? Why did you try to take your own life?"

She hugged me tightly, then held me at arm's length. "I'm sorry I frightened you. It was a stupid thing to do, but last week Dr. Kovacs told me I needed a hysterectomy. Even though he assured me the tumor was benign, I refused to have the surgery. I know I have cervical cancer just like your grandmother and I can't stand the thought of suffering the way she did or being a burden to you. I just wanted to end my life before the pain set in."

I was perplexed. Mother had always had a strong instinct for survival. She had protected me after my father left us and worked hard to keep a roof over our heads and food on the table. She had somehow managed to elude the Nazis and the Arrow Cross during our time in Buda. After I left to join George in Italy, she had kept our little secretarial shop going. Why was she suddenly so sure she was going to die?

"Let me talk to your doctor tomorrow and find out what's really going on," I told her. "I promise I'll tell you the truth, but only if you promise never to give me a scare like that again."

I tried to keep our conversation light and told her about Lynne's bevy of blue ribbons for her riding skills and Lewis's prowess on the soccer field, deliberately avoiding any discussion of George until she asked. Then I poured out my heart, spilling the story of his involvement with Sadie and the generally sad state of my marriage. Instead of commiserating with me, she brightened. "Will you call Dan and tell him I'm in the hospital?" she asked. "As you know, he's been a great help to me through the years. He would surely want to know that you are back in Budapest."

I hesitated, wondering if it was a good idea, then put my worries aside. What harm could come from calling an old friend? Feeling as nervous as a schoolgirl, I dialed his law office. His secretary was abrupt, but put me right through.

"Eva, is it really you after all these years? When can I see you?" My heart began to race.

"Mother asked me to call and tell you she is in the hospital and would like for you to visit," I told him. "She tried to take her own life."

He was as shocked as I had been. "I'll be over right after work. Don't go away."

My heart did somersaults. It had been twenty-four years since I had seen him. Would he be as handsome as I remembered? What would he think of me? I was no longer that young girl he had once loved.

I needn't have worried. As soon as Dan walked into the room, sparks began to fly between us. The years had been kind and he had matured from a good-looking young man into a distinguished gentleman graying at the temples. At that moment, I couldn't remember why I had turned away from him toward George.

Dan pulled me into his arms and hugged me tightly. "You are even more beautiful than I remember, my Eva. I always knew you would come back into my life one day."

He pulled a chair next to mine near Mother's bed and chided her for not calling to tell him she was ill. We stayed for a while, but it soon became apparent that Mother was exhausted and Dan stood up, "Eva, may I drop you off somewhere?" he asked.

"I want to stay with Mother for awhile and make sure...," I said reluctantly.

Mother cut me off mid-sentence "The excitement of having you here has worn me out. I really need to rest now. Run on, you two. I'll see you in the morning."

She didn't have to urge me further. I was exhausted after the long flight and the sleepless night before I left. I also needed time to make sense of the strange emotions I felt over seeing Dan again.

We hadn't progressed far down the hall when I saw a doctor striding toward us. The name on his identification badge read "Ernst Kovacs."

I thrust out my hand. "I'm Eva Friedlander, Margaret Dukes' daughter," I told him. I've just come from visiting my mother who tells me she's terrified that she has cancer. Is it true?"

"Just the opposite," he replied. "I feel certain the tumor is benign. The surgery I've recommended is entirely preemptive. Will you convince her that her condition is not critical and that she should have the surgery before the status changes?"

"Of course," I promised. Before saying our goodbyes, we discussed the best way to alleviate Mother's fears. Dr. Kovacs assured me he would see her on his rounds in the morning and we could discuss options.

Dan carried my suitcase with one hand and hooked his other through the crook of my arm. "Where are you staying, Eva? Should I take you to your Mother's apartment or to a hotel near here?"

"I'm not sure. Would you mind taking me by her apartment so I can pick up a few things for her?"

"I'm happy to take you anywhere."

The ride to the apartment felt surprisingly natural, as if I had made this trip one-thousand times before with Dan behind the wheel. I had the feeling that he felt the same. As we walked up the familiar steps to the apartment, memories washed over me. Becoming engaged to Dan. His internment in the Ukraine. Our escape to Buda. Life on the run. The Soviets' attack in the basement. George.

Tentatively, I turned the key in the lock and pushed the door open, shocked at the condition of the small apartment. Mother had always been scrupulously neat, but the bed was unmade, there were dishes in the sink and a pile of laundry was heaped on a living room chair. Even her beloved plants were withering from lack of water. In fact, the only objects in the room that looked as if they had been dusted in the last few months were the photographs of the children and me. We were staring at the face of depression. How lonely and sad her life must be in this tired little place.

"I can't bear for you to stay here," Dan said, looking around. "Let me take you to dinner and help you find a convenient hotel near the hospital."

Before I could answer a grateful, "yes," Dan picked up Mother's phone and called his wife. "I'm going to be tied up in the office with a client until late," he told her. "Don't wait up for me." He placed the receiver back in its cradle, then turned to me and shrugged. "She never waits up for me anyway. The only thing I find to eat when I get home is a cold sandwich waiting in the refrigerator."

I didn't put up any resistance to Dan's suggestion to go to a hotel. The thought of remaining at Mother's dirty, depressing little apartment was impossible. Once I found time to clean, I would think about it. Dan and I hastily gathered up a few pairs of Mother's pajamas, her toothbrush, hairbrush and robe, threw them into a small valise. As we locked the door behind us. I shivered. "It's hard to imagine her living like this," I told him. "When I was growing up, the house was immaculate."

Dan suggested a small boutique hotel with a decent restaurant that was within walking distance from the hospital. Once I checked in and dropped my bags on the bed, we walked down the stairs to the restaurant. We found a quiet table in the corner and as I was looking the menu over, Dan took it out of my hand. "We'll have two Chicken Paprikas, my friend's favorite Hungarian meal," he told the waitress. "She's just returned after a very long absence."

Isn't that just like Dan to remember my favorite meal after all these years? I thought.

During dinner, we talked about Mother, the flight, and my children, then lingered over espressos. "Tell me about your life," I said. "Mother tells me that you have your own law firm now, but I know nothing else. How is your wife? Do you have children?"

"Suzsi is fine, but we don't have much of a life together," he said. "You must know that I married her on the rebound after you and George left for Italy. It was a huge mistake and I'm afraid our only daughter is paying for it. She's become extremely rebellious, primarily because her mother and I don't see eye to eye on how to mete out discipline. Suzsi lets her do whatever she wants and it's created quite a rift between us."

I could see the pain in Dan's eyes when he talked of his family, but his entire demeanor changed when he described his work defending Austrian clients who had legal issues with the Hungarian government. "I spend as much time in Vienna as I can," he said. "It's become a haven for me, much like our boat house on the Danube where I can go rowing to my heart's content. Will you come with me when your mother feels better?" He picked up my left hand and twirled my wedding band, subconsciously wanting me to remove all signs of that bondage.

I left his unasked question unanswered and stood up. "I didn't sleep at all on the plane and I need to get some rest before I see Mother early tomorrow morning," I said. "Will you come by the hospital to help me convince her to have the surgery?" Once again, his hug said it all.

The next morning, I had every intention of getting to the hospital before Dr. Kovacs arrived, but as it turned out, I overslept and we arrived simultaneously. It took some tall talking from both of us before she would agree to the surgery.

"I'll do it on the condition that you stay with me until I'm strong enough to be alone," she said.

"Not only will I stay until you are stronger, I'm going to take you back to Atlanta with me to recuperate," I told her. "George and the children can hardly wait to see you."

That evening, when George and I talked, I told him that the surgery was scheduled the following week.

"When do you think you can you come home?" he asked.

"It's way too early to tell," I hedged. "I'll have a better idea after her operation."

The days following Mother's successful surgery were glorious for Dan and me. We spent long evenings lingering over wine and dinner in dark, quiet restaurants or strolling down Budapest's tree-lined streets admiring the meticulously restored mansions.

"Budapest is even more beautiful than it was before the war, but I miss some of the old places and the old crowd," I told him. "So many died during the time you were in the Ukraine."

As the weeks passed and Mother's health improved, Dan and I became more brazen about being seen together in public. When actor friends offered him tickets to the theater for an opening night performance, he invited me instead of his wife. We even went backstage after the performance where he introduced me as his "bride." I was dumbfounded. I was also touched.

"Your friends all know you're married. Aren't you worried they will report back to Suzsi that you were here with me?"

"She wouldn't care," he said. "We live separate lives these days, and besides, Europeans are much more liberal about things like that than Americans."

Unlike the total lack of communication in my marriage, Dan and I could talk for hours about anything and everything. We reminisced about our romance, old friends, and family. We argued about history and politics. When I confided that George was having an affair, he said, "Suzsi isn't having an affair, as far as I know, but we haven't slept together in years. I often dream about what it would have been like if you and I had married. I wish I had made love to you just one time."

It seemed an easy transition to stroll toward my hotel room where we lay in one another's arms all night, something that had been denied us when we were young. I never wanted him to leave. And for the next few weeks, we parted only long enough for him to go to work and for me to spend time with Mother. Each night we had dinner together, then headed back to my hotel room. One evening, Dan took my hand and pressed it against his cheek. "I have meetings with clients in Vienna next week," he said. "Please come with me. Vienna is so lovely this time of year."

My eyes filled with tears. "As close as it is to Budapest, I've never seen Vienna and would so love to see it with you, but I can't leave Mother alone right now. She's improving physically but still seems fragile emotionally. Can you put off your trip for a few weeks so we have more time together?"

"Sadly, no, but I'll try to finish up quickly and I'll call you every evening."

Dan was gone for three long days; true to his word, he called each evening to discuss his cases and tell me how much he missed me. Once back in Budapest, he rearranged his calendar and delayed everything except court appearances in order to spend as much time with me as he could. Mother beamed each time we walked into the room together. "This is just like old times before the war interrupted your romance," she said. "Isn't it wonderful to have Eva back in Budapest?"

I lingered for several weeks after Mother fully regained her strength, dreading to return home to George. If it hadn't been for being desperate to see my children, I would likely have stayed indefinitely.

George called nearly every evening and at the end of the conversation he always asked, "When are you coming home? The children miss you."

I made up one excuse after the other. "Mother isn't ready to live on her own yet," or "I'm working on her exit visa and we can't fly home until she receives it."

Occasionally, he peppered me with questions. "Have you seen any of the old crowd or gone by my parents' old house? What about your old flame, Dan?" It was a rhetorical question because George already knew the answer. On several occasions Dan and I had run into a friend of George's who just "happened" to be in the same restaurant or cafe we frequented. It was too coincidental to be happenstance and I felt sure George had asked him to check up on me and report back.

"Of course, I've seen Dan. He's continued to see Mother through the years and is using his legal connections to expedite Mother's visa. She's agreed to a visit but wants to keep her apartment here so she can return when she's ready. I'm trying to talk her into staying permanently."

Lewis seemed matter of fact about my long absence, but every time we talked Lynne begged me to come home. "I'm making you something, Mommy," she told me one night when George passed the phone to her. "Don't you want to come home and see what it is?" I explained that I missed them all terribly, but needed to stay with Grandma until she was better.

Each time I talked to either of the children, I was overcome with guilt. In truth, I felt worse about leaving them for so long than my affair with Dan. Hadn't George been fooling around with Sadie for years? In fact, it was highly likely that he was seeing her even more frequently since I was out of the country.

To make some practical use of my time in Budapest, Dan and I strolled in and out of antique shops buying paintings for the ADAC showroom. I had a dozen or more shipped home, primarily so George would know I was using my time productively. Shopping with Dan was a pleasure. While George always had something critical to say about my selections, Dan repeatedly complimented my ability to discern a valuable antique from a fine imitation. He also asked me to help him choose a landscape for his office. In the end, he decided on a view of the Danube's multiple bridges, a sight we admired from a small café we frequented. It had been a long time since a man had made me feel so competent.

Mother's visa arrived after a six-week wait and I reluctantly purchased plane tickets for a week hence. I had tears in my eyes when I told Dan of our pending departure.

"Of course you must return to Atlanta for your children, but you have to know that we were always meant to live our lives together. It may be twenty-four years later than I planned, but we still have many wonderful years ahead of us."

I nodded, too filled with emotion to speak and snuggled close to him.

"Regardless of what happens, I plan to divorce Suzsi and pray you will divorce George and return home to Budapest so we can be a family," he said.

The day before our flight to Atlanta, Dan and I drove to Szentendre, a lovely artist's colony on the bank of the Danube north of Budapest. Along the way, we stopped at a little café on Pilis Hill where we listened to gypsy music and lingered over glasses of crisp Hungarian wine.

"Leaving George will be extremely hard," I told him. "I know he won't give up easily and Lewis will be terribly unhappy about leaving his father and his friends. I can't just walk in and announce I want a divorce so I can move to Hungary with the children."

"I know, my love. It will be agonizing, but you'll eventually be able to change the course of your life so we can have a new beginning. I'm extremely anxious to meet your children and help them adjust to a European lifestyle. Promise me you will begin steps for a separation soon."

When Dan put us on the plane the next day, he and I clung to one another, hating to part. Mother was in tears. I had no idea whether it was because she was leaving her homeland or because I was leaving Dan behind once again.

As the plane took off and we settled in our seats, she turned to me and said. "All these years I've prayed that you and Dan would reconcile so you could move back to Budapest," she said. "Now that it looks like it may happen, I'm torn. You've had such a beautiful life in America and been so successful. How will you bear to leave it all behind?"

I leaned my head back against the seat and closed my eyes. How, indeed?

Once the plane landed, I jumped into life full force, taking Lewis to karate, Lynne to horseback riding lessons and both to religious school at our synagogue where Lewis was studying for his Bar Mitzvah. During my long absence, work had piled up at the ADAC showroom and it took some adjustment to get back in the groove.

Despite my joy at being with Lynne and Lewis again, I chafed at the bit. My six weeks in Budapest, had been so carefree and happy. My handsome Dan had called me "beautiful" and "brilliant." George, on the other hand, was on the offensive. He hinted that my visit had been far more about re-igniting my romance with Dan than caring for Mother and he was also angry that I had not spent time with *his* friends. Oddly, I didn't feel guilty either over the affair or avoiding his friends.

Dan's secret letters to my post office box and phone calls to my office phone sustained me during those early months. We were extremely careful not to tip our hands before coming to a decision about our future. My cousin,

Gyorgyi, a great admirer of Dan's, became our post office. I put my letters to Dan in a double envelope and addressed the outer one to her. When they arrived, she'd call so he could pick them up. In turn, he passed his letters to me through Gyorgyi so she could write in her return address, then mail them to my post office box.

A prolific, passionate writer, Dan wrote letters full of longing. He constantly reminded me of our wonderful evenings together and our dreams to turn our lives in totally different directions. "Every move I make and everything I do reminds me of you," he wrote. "I pretend that you are still staying at the little hotel around the corner from the hospital and that I will see you in the evening." His romantic nature was integral in every letter and his understated humor made me chuckle every time I re-read them. I lived for the almost daily correspondence and it sustained me through many rough spots. Dan offered an escape from my unhappy marriage and hope for a brighter future.

Yet, months passed and, despite his pleas, I didn't make any attempt to divorce or even separate from George. Truth be told, I think my affair with Dan was simply a lovely interlude. The reality of uprooting Lynne and Lewis and returning to Budapest was just too difficult. On days that I vacillated, I remembered how I had felt when my father left Mother and me for Magda and, despite Sadie's shadow looming behind me, I couldn't bring myself to do the same thing to my children.

There were also other issues — the same ones Marta and I talked about when Lynne and I stayed in her home after the strip poker incident. Divorce, though entirely doable in the 1970s, still carried a stigma. And despite my success, the financial loss would have been considerable.

After my father left us, Mother and I struggled to make ends meet. Re-creating that shaky scenario for my children was unthinkable. I wanted security and a college education for them — things I had not been afforded. How could I risk that for my own selfish desires?

In addition, our similar experiences during the war years also played a part. George and I had been raised six-thousand miles from American shores and had a bond born from our immigration and assimilation. It proved to be one I couldn't bear to break. Looking back, it was one of those "could of, should of moments" I let slip through my fingers. Had I really fallen in love with Dan again or was I just trying to get even with George for his perpetual affair with Sadie?

I didn't want to burden Mother with my indecision, so I poured my heart out to Edit who was by that time living happily with her new husband in Caracas. During one of our conversations, Edit summed it up, "You and Dan toyed with one another," she said. "It was fun while it lasted, but I'm not sure either of you truly believed there was a future."

Unlike Mrs. Friedlander, Mother set about fitting into our lives and embracing the chaos of two busy, active children plus a menagerie of Friedlander family pets. She was usually the first to arise in the morning and was in the kitchen preparing breakfast when George woke up. She played him as adeptly as a virtuoso violinist. "George, you look especially handsome this morning," she'd say, or, "You selected the perfect tie to go with that suit." He loved the flattery and left the house whistling. He also adored her cooking and she went out of her way to prepare his favorite dishes and have a delicious meal waiting for us when we came home from work.

Although Mother could both see and feel the tension between George and me and easily understood our arguments in Hungarian about Sadie, I tried not to involve her. And she displayed amazing restraint by not saying "I told you so." But I knew she was thinking it. If I complimented her deft treatment of George, she would say, "Instead of fighting, you should try flattery. If I hadn't harped on your father about his business failures, he might never have taken up with Magda."

I knew she was right, but in my defense, I felt I had tried everything — silent submission, self-blame, fighting, emotional distancing. Nothing had worked. And though I tried as hard as I could to take her advice, words of false flattery stuck in my craw.

The lack of a separate bedroom for Mother only added to the tension in the household. Because we only had three bedrooms, Lynne was sharing Lewis's room, leaving hers for Mother. Lewis, a sports fanatic, hated her dolls and dresses taking up space needed for "guy stuff" and Lynne missed her horse posters and chatting on the phone with friends out of his earshot. Since neither had a sliver of privacy, the arrangement also made it difficult for them to invite friends over to spend the night.

Two years after her arrival, Mother broached the subject of moving. "I've decided to remain in Atlanta permanently near you and the children, but I need my own apartment," she said. "And you and George need your house back so you can make a decision about your marriage. You know how I adore Dan, but the decision to stay with George is yours alone. Besides, Lewis is growing up and needs his own space. So does Lynne."

I couldn't disagree. The children fought constantly, something they had rarely done when they had their own rooms. Besides, although she never complained, Mother must have found the lack of privacy difficult after living alone for so many years.

A major issue in finding her a suitable apartment was finances. She had no income and George and I couldn't take on the added expenses of supporting another household. Luckily, I found her an apartment in the federally subsidized Lutheran Towers on Juniper Street. Even though she was not yet an American citizen, she was eligible at age seventy-five for a small social security check and food stamps. I supplemented the rest out of my earnings. I suspect because she was accustomed to living frugally, she managed her finances beautifully and occasionally took the National Bank to task for small errors they made on her statements. She handled it so diplomatically that they went out of their way to accommodate her.

Mother's departure from our house seemed to exacerbate George's unexplained absences from home. We sometimes began the day bickering and ended it on the same note. The same fight repeated one-thousand times, followed by days of stony silence.

As the tension in the house mounted, the children began acting out. One day after school, Lewis went on the attack. "Why are you always mad with Dad and why doesn't he ever come home for dinner any more? Does he have to work that hard?" My vague answer didn't appease him and I watched worry lines march across his young forehead as he stomped off.

Lynne, on the other hand, clearly identified with me and barely spoke to her dad unless he demanded it. After a whopper of a fight between George and me, she begged once again, "Get a divorce, Mommy. We don't need

Daddy." I grieved over the fact that at such a young age, she fully understood that her father and I shared a house, but not our lives.

Thankfully, when it came to the children's problems, we were always on the same page, particularly during their teen years. Lewis scared us to death when he ran his mini-bike into a ditch on busy Northside Drive and the police brought him home. Thankfully, he wasn't injured, but he had scraped up his arms and legs so badly he limped around for days. As a punishment for leaving without permission, we refused to have the mini-bike repaired or to buy him a new one. It wasn't until months later that he confessed he had flown out of the house that night without permission during one of our long fights. "I couldn't stand hearing the two of you yell at one another any longer," he told us. "I had to get out or explode."

Lynne rebelled by crawling out her window and sitting on the edge of the roof to smoke. We strongly suspected that she also used it as a way to sneak out of the house to meet her friends and boyfriends after we were asleep, but we could never prove it. Years later she told us, "I jumped from the ledge to the backyard, then snuck through the gate and down the street where my friends picked me up." In retrospect, I'm just as glad I didn't know she was gallivanting around Atlanta during the wee hours. I would have been worried sick.

It was odd how George and I could come together to deal with the children and then have ferocious fights on the same day. I have little recollection of George's brutality, but Lynne clearly remembers seeing bruises on my arms and face from his tirades and vicious shaking. She also remembers hearing her father yell, "You provoked me!" and the crack of the door when he slammed it.

I suppose that on one level I bought into it because I felt guilty about my affair with Dan, but George had always been a master of persuasion, a man who could talk logically on both sides of an argument. It was this very same skill that saved his life over and over during the war. Likely, he felt guilty over his torrid affair with Sadie and deflected it by heaping the blame on me. I didn't understand until years later that shouldering the blame is one of the classic symptoms of an abused wife. Likely, his inability to remain faithful had far more to do with his insatiable sexual needs, the frustration of never achieving the success he thought was rightfully his, and his psychological wiring.

Years later, my wise daughter summed it up well. "He pretends to be a big man by driving expensive cars and wearing Armani suits, and to the outside world he is. But it's all artificial. At home, he has to face the reality that he has failed as a husband and he doesn't like what he sees. He becomes extremely insecure and is terrified of losing you."

In public, I put on a "happy wife" face and he was the solicitous "perfect" husband. When we were alone, we descended either into détente or all out war, and the further our marriage disintegrated, the better it worked for Sadie. George's clothes lived at the house — he didn't.

I reached the boiling point when George walked in after midnight for the fifth night in a row. "Where have you been this time?" I shrieked. "Do you think this house is a hotel where you can come and go as you please? You lie to me about what you are doing, cheat on me with Sadie — and then have the nerve to deny you're having

an affair when everyone tells me that they see the two of
you all over town. Do you think I'm stupid?"

George shouted a few obscenities and clenched his
fists as red, hot spikes of anger flamed on his cheeks. He
looked ready to explode. I recall thinking I had pushed
him too far and had better get out of his sight, so I turned
my back and retreated to the porch where Lynne was
sitting on the wicker couch trying to study. I don't
remember the incident clearly, but Lynne tells me that
George followed and shoved me so hard I landed on the
brick floor and hit my head and cheek hard enough to
black out. "He picked up our clunky dial telephone and
came charging at you again," she said. "I tried to fend him
off with my feet and yelled for Lewis who came running.
Dad must have been frightened when he saw your eyes
roll back in your head and he backed off."

With maturity far beyond his sixteen years, Lewis
took charge and told Lynne to run and get an icepack for
my face. I regained consciousness a few minutes later and
have vague memories of my head in Lynne's lap.

"Mom, we need to get you to the Piedmont Hospital
emergency room right away," Lewis said. "You're going
to need some stitches in that cheek."

I looked from his face to Lynne's and tried to touch
my cheek. When I saw George standing in the doorway,
his face paler than the lab coat he frequently wore, I
recalled the beginning of our fight, but nothing else.

I have no recollection of the car ride, but Lynne
described the scene in great detail. "You sat next to me on
the back seat and your teeth were chattering like crazy.
Lewis and I had picked up enough medical information
from Dad to worry you were going into shock. I was still
so scared even after we got there, I wouldn't move from

your side. The doctors finally pried the ice pack out of my hands so they could take a look at your cheek, but I pitched a fit when they wouldn't let Lewis and me go with you to get an x-ray. Afterwards, they let us stay in the room while the plastic surgeon put in stitches."

Chapter 17

In the days and weeks that followed the incident, George was more contrite than I had ever seen him and insisted on going with me to have the stitches removed. "I don't know what came over me," he said. "I must have snapped. I swear it will never happen again." In an act of contrition, he even agreed to go to counseling again, this time to a psychiatrist of his choosing.

For a time, we went separately and I poured out my heart about George's affair with Sadie, his constant absences from home, his fierce anger and my own inability to curb my temper. Sometimes I cried. Sometimes I paced the room. Other times I ranted and raved. "He says I provoke him," I told her, "and I guess I do."

"I seriously doubt it's your fault," she said. "Regardless of blame, George has no right to lay a hand on you in anger. Ever. Your mistake was not stopping the business relationship with Sadie before it escalated into an affair."

I was taken back. Was she, too, putting the blame on my shoulders? Should a wife mistrust every interaction her husband has with another woman? In George's case, the answer was "yes." But that was a lesson I hadn't yet learned when Sadie first entered the picture. Deep down, I'm still not sure what came first, the business partnership or their affair. Was George sincere about finding ways for the family to prosper, or was he just looking for a legitimate excuse to spend time alone with Sadie?

During George's sessions with the psychiatrist, he complained about me. "She spends too much time and attention on the children and her antique business, and doesn't have enough left for me," he said. "Everything was fine when Eva stayed home with Lewis, but the moment Lynne was born, she gave one-hundred percent of her attention to caring for the two of them and left me out in the cold."

With the psychiatrist's help, we tried to hash out our differences in joint sessions. I admitted that I doted on the children and put my emphasis on raising them. I promised to be more solicitous of his feelings. Other than apologizing for the rage that had sent me to the hospital, he categorically refused to admit he was wrong in any area — whether the affair with Sadie, which he still denied, or his violent outbursts. In frustration over the lack of progress and the mounting hourly bills, I suggested we try seeing a counselor at Jewish Family Services, an organization that used a sliding fee scale.

The deep rift between us obviously affected the children too and our new counselor asked us to include them in our sessions. A few months after we began, however, the therapist said "I don't see much hope for improvement. George, apparently you feel faultless and are unwilling to take responsibility for your actions. Until you shoulder part of the blame and admit to your long standing affair, I can't help you."

His face turned flame red, just as it had the night he shoved me to the ground. "You're crazy," he said. "You're all crazy. I'm the only sane one in this group." With that, he stormed out the door.

Despite his righteous declaration that he was without fault, he behaved like a contrite man and came home for dinner nearly every night during the months that followed. He also showered me with compliments and occasionally brought flowers or candy. During a business trip to Italy, he called nightly and brought me a lovely twenty-four carat gold bracelet with a smaller version for Lynne.

I was thrilled at the 180-degree turnabout which I attributed to his realization that his marriage was worth saving. After years of acrimony, the George who wooed me with lovemaking and impressed me with his knowledge of art, music, and history had reappeared. On a dare from a friend, he purchased some art supplies, set up an easel in his office and drew a charcoal and pencil portrait of me wearing a large picture hat. The resemblance is remarkable. He also copied an oil masterpiece by Thomas Gainsborough so accurately that Lewis begged me to give it to him. For a man who had never had a single art lesson, it was an incredible feat.

For the better part of the following year, we settled into a relatively normal lifestyle. Gradually, George worked his way back into the children's good graces. If he were still seeing Sadie, then it must have been during the daylight hours because he rarely missed spending evenings at home. We took a wonderful family vacation to Jamaica with the children and another to Ibiza, an incredibly beautiful island on the eastern edge of Spain to visit our dear friends from Rome, Pista and Agnes Herman. We even managed to go to Miami by ourselves on several occasions. Once, George said excitedly, "Let's sell the house in Atlanta and move the business here where there is perpetual sunshine, fresh seafood and ocean as far as the eye can see."

I looked at him askance. "I love coming here for brief spells, but certainly don't want to pull the children out of school or give up the connections I've made in the antique business and the wonderful associates you've made in the chemical community," I told him. "Besides, seeing all these old people with their weathered skin reminds me of an elephant's burial ground. The case is closed."

George pouted for a while, but didn't bring it up again except to insist that we spend every vacation in Miami. I would have preferred a different location at least occasionally, but feeling guilty about quashing his idea to relocate, I bowed to his wishes. I've often wondered if I had reacted differently and we had moved to Miami if George's philandering would have ended.

One holiday in Miami sans children was like a second honeymoon and we seemed to rekindle the long extinguished flame. Always the adventurer, George rented a small raft and a fishing rod and paddled solo out into the ocean. Somehow, he snagged a small hammerhead shark and dragged it aboard without tipping the raft. "What in the world are we going to do with it? Make shark fin soup?"

George laughed. "I want to take him home to show our little animal lover, Lynne. She'll be fascinated."

My worry over Lynne's reaction to the dead shark paled when we returned home and found Lewis and his "Dukes of Hazard" star friend, Byron Cherry, ankle deep in Georgia red clay in our back yard, shovels in hand. "We're building you and Dad a three-level koi pond," he said excitedly. "You're going to love it."

Initially, we were annoyed about all the mud, mess, and expense, but before long, everyone in the family became involved in the project and the koi pond became our favorite spot to cook out and entertain business associates and friends. It also gave me a peaceful refuge when I needed an escape from my marital woes.

One evening not long after we returned to Atlanta from Miami, George sat down next to me on the den sofa and took my hand in his. "Promise that you'll hear me out before you say no," he said. "I have an idea about Sadie."

The very mention of her name made my blood pressure rise, but for once, I kept my mouth closed. "I'm tired of her interference and advances," he continued. "No matter what I say or do, I can't get her to stop pursuing me."

My thoughts careened like a car out of control. Just who had been pursuing whom? Also, this was the first time George had even acknowledged that he and Sadie had anything other than a business relationship.

"What did you have in mind?" I asked cautiously.

"I'd like to introduce her to my friend, Ben. If they take a shine to one another, it will get her off *our* backs, but I need your cooperation."

I didn't know what to make of the wild idea. On one hand, it could have teeth. Ben owned a successful pharmacy in northeast Atlanta, the first one in the city to remain open all night. Though he was certainly not a ladies man like George, he was naively charming and an accomplished violinist with the Atlanta Symphony. He was also a little unconventional, a quality that might appeal to Sadie's Bohemian side.

"She's made plenty of money as a realtor," George continued, "but Ben inherited a sizeable amount recently and a little added wealth never hurt anyone." I couldn't help but smile. Despite George's brilliance, talents and appeal, he had never achieved the success to which he felt entitled, and was continually frustrated over all the "could of, should of's" in his life — failure to demand recourse from the Italian government for not rescuing him from Andrassy 60; waffling on medical school until it was too late; his failure to amass great wealth.

Despite the distaste of sharing a meal with Sadie, I agreed to call Ben to invite him to join us for dinner at Veni Vidi Vici. I categorically refused to call Sadie. I would love to have listened in on that conversation. She must have been shocked and hurt that George wanted to introduce her to another man.

The day of our staged dinner, my stomach did such a jitterbug I was sorely tempted to back out. Would I be able to hold my tongue and be civil to Sadie in front of Ben? At the last moment, I decided to put on my most becoming dress and go — but not before I fortified myself with a healthy gulp of vermouth.

George's scheme worked better than my wildest dreams. Sadie and Ben immediately became an item and married a few months later. I was thrilled. A newlywed wouldn't cheat on her brand new husband, would she? Obviously, the answer remained to be seen, but in the meantime, Sadie was out of my hair. Perhaps George and I could repair the deep rift in our marriage permanently.

"We're entering a new phase of our lives," I told Edit during our weekly call. "I think we might make it after all."

"I don't know if this leopard can change his spots," she cautioned. "Don't get too complacent. Sadie may be out of the picture for now, but there are plenty of other attractive women in Atlanta."

Chapter 18

I paid Edit's warning little heed because in addition to the improvement in our relationship, our finances were also on the upswing. Custom Chemicals was practically running itself. The only problem was that George had too much time on his hands and began exploring business opportunities out of his field to broaden his reach in the community.

One investment idea came from an old French friend, Henri, who had worked in the French Underground while George was working with the Zionist Underground. They found a connection while both were attending a scientific conference in Las Vegas. He was an unbelievable marketer who came up with one money-making idea after another. "His latest venture is a deserted gold mine with a large untapped vein. He wants us to come in as full partners. What do you think?"

"No way," I replied. "I greatly respect Henri's reputation as a recruiter for the French Underground during the war, but most of his wild ideas seem like pyramid schemes to me. What guarantee do you have that he has really found gold?"

"He's showed me the geologic surveys and it looks promising," George said. "I'm calling from the lobby of the Sands Hotel and it's too noisy here to talk. We'll talk about it when I come home."

I was ready to hang up when George said, "Wait. Who do you think just sat down at the slot machine next to me? Without pausing for an answer, he said, "It's the comedian Joey Bishop. He's headlining at the Sands. 'Here, Joey, say hello to my wife, Eva.'"

The next voice I heard on the phone was unmistakably Joey's. "Eva," he said with a thick tongue. "George is so drunk he just slid under the table."

When George came home a few days later, he again approached me about the gold mine, but I could tell he was not totally convinced of its merits. Apparently, the venture was too risky even for George.

He soon became excited about another of Henri's investments — a string of condos in a posh area of Lisbon. "He's invited me to go on the next junket for free," he said. "He's marketing his idea by luring investors with free trips to Portugal's gorgeous coast. Once they see the property, they fall in love and let loose their money."

I shrugged. "Ours is tied up in two businesses now, Custom Chemicals and the ADAC showroom. Isn't that enough?"

George toyed with the idea for months before backing off. Though the decision not to invest in the gold mines was a good one since they never produced enough gold to justify the investment, Henri's condos sold like hotcakes to both Americans and Europeans. Both he and his partners made a killing — something George never let me forget.

Still, the passion to further his reach didn't end. Several months later George came home with a spring in his step and another business proposal. "I just met a brilliant business woman named Marjorie Jones who owns a very lucrative modeling school," he said. "After the students complete her course, she helps the most attractive ones land contracts at top agencies in New York. She's ready to expand her business into a nationwide franchise and has offered us a golden opportunity to get in on the ground floor. I think we ought to do it."

I immediately saw red. Another business venture with yet another "Sadie" was the last thing I wanted. I put my hands on my hips and poked my finger in his chest.

"You tell me that Custom Chemicals is finally showing a healthy profit. Why should we risk that success on another venture? Isn't one company enough to satisfy you?"

George remained uncharacteristically calm. "I know how you hate for me to bring up her name, but our business transactions with Sadie were very profitable and gave me the seed money for Custom Chemicals," he said. "Will you just meet Marjorie and keep an open mind? I think you'll like her and I promise I won't invest a penny if you don't feel it's a good move financially. After all, we are *partners* in everything."

237

It was an odd comment coming from George who had never made me a partner in any of his business dealings — or even in our own household. Each time I asked for information about his business or our savings, he brushed me off claiming I needn't worry because he was taking care of everything. Suddenly, he was calling me his partner? It didn't make sense at the time. I didn't realize until much later how skillfully that one word had turned my anger upside down.

"All right," I agreed reluctantly. "I'll meet her, but I don't promise to take to the idea."

Before our rendezvous with Marjorie, I prodded him for details. "If we decide to go into business with her, how much do you want to invest? Has your accountant taken a look at her books? How much control will we have in the decision-making process?" His answers were so vague I had the uneasy feeling that it was already a done deal. Did he just want me to rubber stamp the venture?

We met over cocktails at the Buckhead Ritz-Carlton and when Marjorie walked in, I was taken aback. Though she had the long, lean figure of a former model, she lacked the requisite beauty. Her inky black hair hung listlessly to her shoulders, emphasizing her almost masculine features, and her handshake was so forceful that my fingers ached. Although she seemed the epitome of a successful modern businesswoman — traits George admired in everyone but me — she went against type for a man who had always been attracted to voluptuous women like Sadie. I was even surprised he wanted to match wits with such a strong woman, one who would likely not be amenable to his every suggestion.

Drinks led to dinner and on through dessert. I peppered Marjorie with questions about the business. "When did you open? How many students do you have? How many do you accept in each class? Are you the only instructor?"

She seemed forthright in her answers. She had been in business for five years and her students now numbered around 30 a course. Aspiring models completed three courses. "We've had a waiting list every session for the last year," she said. "I'm anxious to expand while the interest is so high. New York is the place to begin. If we make it there, the sky's the limit and we can franchise agencies all over the country." She made it sound like such a sure thing that by the time we finished our second cup of coffee, George and I were in the modeling business.

Marjorie and George were an odd combination. For one thing, she towered over him. But she also played him as adeptly as "Satchmo" tooted his famous brass horn. He seemed to go along with everything she said, even her invitation to be one of the speakers at the Easter Sunrise Services at Georgia's famous Stone Mountain State Park. He was thrilled.

"Just think what an honor it is for a Jewish refugee from Hungary to speak in front of thousands of people at Easter services. You must come to hear me."

"What a crazy idea, I said. "Easter is one of the holiest days of the year for Christians. What could a Jew possibly say that would be appropriate for such an occasion?"

He sputtered for a few minutes. "I haven't given it much thought yet, but I think I'll talk about the universal theme that runs through all religions, a Power that guides our lives and gives us faith."

We argued about it for weeks. He had no intention of backing out and I was adamant that it was inappropriate. In the end, I refused to go.

George came home from the service all aglow. "It was really something," he boasted. "There were thousands of people at both the top of the mountain and down at the base where I spoke," he said. "I was the only non-Christian on the program and Marjorie said the crowd hung on every word."

Over the course of the next few months, I suspected more than just a business relationship between the two, but a chill came over the household every time I asked if Marjorie had expanded into the New York modeling market yet. "It's going well, just slowly," George assured me. "Getting a business license in New York and finding office space takes time. I promise we'll see a profit soon after it opens."

Not long thereafter, a fat official-looking letter from one of the top criminal attorneys in Atlanta arrived in the mail. I thought it was odd, but simply put it on George's desk. The next day while I was dusting, I saw the open letter still sitting in the same spot. We had an unspoken rule that neither opened the other's personal mail, but that letter drew me in like quicksand. I walked away twice before being sucked in.

The first sentence made my stomach churn. The attorney wrote that he was representing Marjorie in a lawsuit she was going to file over George's "life-threatening" behavior. There were few details, but the meaning was clear. George had apparently lost his temper just as he had the time his shove sent me to the hospital. Had he struck her? Had she been injured?

I didn't know what to do with this ill-gotten information. If I told George I had read his mail, he would surely fly into a rage. If I didn't, the entire episode – whatever it was — could implode our lives.

Somehow, I managed to bide my time waiting for him to confess. With each passing day, my patience frayed a little more. Finally, a very agitated George came home during the day while the children were at school and thrust the letter in my lap. "Read this," he said.

I read it slowly, as if I had never seen it before. "What does this mean for us?" I asked. "What have you done this time?"

George began tentatively. "Marjorie and I met for lunch two or three times a week to discuss her progress in New York," he said.

"Was she running a model agency or a brothel?" I asked sarcastically.

He ignored my snide remark.

"Every time I asked for an update, she gave one excuse after the other. Either her 'people' couldn't find the ideal location or there was a problem obtaining a business license. I was afraid she had cooked the books to lure us in as investors without really planning to expand."

"On the day in question," he said, "we went to Chattahoochee River Park to walk and talk, only it ended up in a shouting match. She refused to turn over the books to my accountant and I accused her of cheating. I demanded that she return our investment immediately. When she laughed in my face, I lost my temper. I suppose I was rougher than I intended to be because she fell down screaming that I was trying to push her into the river.

People came running from all directions so I took off for the parking lot. I'm not even sure how she got home."

I sat in stony silence, refusing to answer George's pleas for understanding. Finally, he begged. "Please believe me. It isn't as it seems. My relationship with Marjorie was strictly business."

"Business? What kind of business," I yelled. "You invested *our* joint savings for what? Another expensive romp in bed? I hope she was worth it."

I clamped my mouth shut, afraid that if I went too far, he might hit me again. And this time, the children weren't home to help me.

"You don't fully understand," he said. "This is not just about an affair. If the case goes to trial, she'll accuse me not only of trying to push her into the river but of sexual assault. We could lose everything."

"And just what do you want me to do about it?" I asked. "I hardly think she would listen to the pleas of the wronged wife."

"We have to move fast to protect our assets," he said. "My business is incorporated so it's safe, but our personal savings and house are another matter. I'm begging you to go with me to our attorney tomorrow so we can transfer everything we own into your name alone. Marjorie won't be able to touch it. We have to protect what we've worked so hard for."

It was the ultimate irony. George had always insisted that his name alone should appear on all our joint investments, including the house. In my European naiveté about the role of wives as subordinates in a marriage, I had gone along for years, but as I became involved in business ventures of my own, my views changed. Despite proving that I was entirely capable of managing the

South's premier antique department at Rich's, as well as my own business at ADAC, I had never been able to convince him to add my name on official documents — regardless of my frequent histrionics.

Now the table had turned. He was begging me to do exactly what I had wanted for some time. Even as I seethed over his inappropriate involvement with yet another businesswoman, I felt great satisfaction at the thought of having the upper hand financially. Revenge, though small, was sweet.

It was also an optimal time to leave the marriage. The house, the car, our investments — all were in my name. George owned nothing. Plus, no one — not my friends or children — could blame me for divorcing a man who was being sued by his former lover. To this day, I don't know why I didn't take advantage of the situation.

The case hung over our heads for months with our law firm and Marjorie's negotiating back and forth. In the end, Marjorie's business went bust — just as George had suspected — and the case collapsed with it. There was plenty of collateral damage. In addition to the further erosion of our marriage, we had lost our initial investment, plus a sizable amount in legal fees. What's more, Custom Chemicals suffered because he was so distracted, first by the modeling school and then by the lawsuit, that he had neglected it at a time when we needed funds for the children's college educations.

"You son of a bitch," I told him on the day we got the news that the agency had closed and Marjorie had fled to the west coast. "You didn't marry Sadie off for the sake of our marriage. You were just bored with her and ready for a new conquest." In truth, I was equally angry with myself. Once again, I could have, should have read the road signs.

~~~~~

Like a ham actor in a Grade B movie, George begged for forgiveness and, for a time, he was on his best behavior. To put Custom Chemicals back on track, he cut his staff to the bone and grabbed the reigns again. He filled in the gaps in his staff by hiring Lynne and Lewis to take over some of the duties whenever they could. Lynne, a high school senior, helped me file on weekends; Lewis pitched in at the plant when he was home on breaks from the University of Georgia.

Despite the animosity between us, George and I were generally on the same page when it came to the children. While Lewis was in high school, George bought an expensive red vintage Corvette in need of massive repairs. It was intended as the ultimate father-son bonding experience, but I secretly felt it was also a bit of a bribe to keep Lewis firmly on his side during our all-too frequent arguments.

Part of the deal was that George asked Lewis to sign a written agreement stating he would only work on the Corvette after school and he couldn't exchange parts or make major repairs without his father's presence and approval. The venture was a total disaster. Instead of it being fun for both, Lewis was surly and disrespectful and the two of them had violent arguments. Time after time, Lewis pushed the envelope and broke every rule. In a fit of rage, or perhaps sanity, George sold the car without telling Lewis who came home from school one day to find the Corvette missing from the driveway.

"Where's my car?" he yelled. "What has Dad done with it?"

I remained mum. "You'll have to talk to your father when he comes home," I said calmly. "This is between the two of you."

That evening, Lewis met his father at the door. "What have you done with my car?" he demanded.

George looked at him coldly. "You broke your contract repeatedly, so I sold it to a fellow chemist as a birthday present for his daughter," he said.

Lewis fumed for weeks, and George sulked over the lost opportunity to work side by side with his son. A few months later, we were shocked to learn that the daughter had been killed in an accident while she was driving the Corvette. We were all grief stricken over the tragedy of losing such a lovely young girl in the very vehicle that Lewis and George had rebuilt.

In its wake, George proposed a second arrangement. If Lewis would save the money he earned working at the plant, he would help him buy another car, albeit a less flashy model that offered more protection. They ended up with an old Volkswagen bus, which Lewis spent endless hours turning into a party car and dating machine — not exactly what George had in mind. Nonetheless, he kept it for many years.

Chapter 19

When George found another lover, I recognized all the signs. His step was a little lighter, his mood brighter, and he took more than the usual time to dress in the morning, changing one tie for another until a puddle of silk dripped off his chair. I strongly suspected that his love interest was his new secretary, Sue, a petite brunette with a lovely figure who was also married with two children — a fact she ignored as adeptly as he did.

I suppose to justify his even longer hours away from home or to broaden his professional reach — or both — he plunged into another business venture. This time it was with U.S. Research Corp., a California-based multi-level company similar to Amway's model of home party sales. George's main job was to develop and manufacture household cleaning products for home use and manage the Atlanta office, which he named Help International Corp. For him, it was the fulfillment of one of his many dreams to develop a line of unique products to be marketed by a legion of entrepreneurial women who would recruit new housewives into the fold.

I had serious reservations. "Amway beat you to the idea," I objected. "Why do you think you can create better products and compete on that level?"

"Amway is exactly why it will work," he explained. "They pioneered the concept and women know that it's a successful marketing plan. With money behind us from California investors, Help International could become a front runner."

No amount of arguing swayed him. The California partners clearly recognized both his talent for creating new cleaning products and his insatiable need for flattery. He became their Golden Boy — a role he relished — the man who developed their most popular product line, Help!

Just as he always wore Armani suits and French silk ties, George didn't stint on furnishings for the new office. He purchased leather chairs and an enormous antique mahogany table for the conference room where he conducted training sessions and sales meetings. Although he checked in with Custom Chemicals daily and worked there at least one day a week, Sue was the pendulum that swung back and forth between the two distinct companies and I helped out by overseeing the billing and collections at the manufacturing operation.

During vacations when Lynne helped in the office, she told me she could feel the sexual electricity between George and Sue. "It made me furious and completely eroded what little respect I had left for him," she told me.

"As if that weren't bad enough, when he met my friend, JoAnne, and me in Venice, he described his sexual prowess with other women in great detail. I was so mortified I could barely look her in the eye. What possible motivation could he have had to embarrass me like that?"

Lewis was also aware of the sizzling affair, but he was always able to shrug off his father's lapses in fidelity that never seemed to daunt his adoration. By that time, I was in an "I don't give a damn" mood and paid little attention. In an act of rebellion, I bought a brand new car to replace my old jalopy without discussing it with George. I simply drove out to Cobb Parkway where dealerships lined the road and pulled into the Chevrolet lot.

"I want to see a new Monte Carlo," I told the salesman, "and I'm ready to buy it today if you give me a good deal." He likely thought he could put one over on me, but I had checked around and done my homework. In the end, I felt proud I had been able to use the same skills I employed with antique dealers to negotiate a fair price, an ability George always negated. As soon as I had the keys in my hand, I called and asked George to meet me out front of his office in half an hour. When I pulled up in my brand new blue and white Monte Carlo, his mouth dropped open.

"Whose car are you driving?" he asked suspiciously.

"Mine, of course. Don't you love the color?"

His face began to redden. "What do you know about buying a car?" he asked. "Why didn't you consult me?"

"You know full well that I've needed a new car for months. Besides, I don't need to ask your permission. I paid for it myself."

George was clearly miffed, but what could he do? The Monte Carlo was a done deal. In truth, I doubt if it made more than a momentary ripple in his mind because he was so involved in U.S. Research he paid little attention to anything else, not Custom Chemical, not even Lewis.

Almost nightly, we had heated arguments about his failure to prioritize between Custom Chemicals and Help, Inc. "Why can't you see it?" I accused. "We have our entire livelihood tied up in Custom Chemicals, yet you're devoting most of your time to this new business. Why don't you concentrate on bolstering the one that has been so successful and is the mainstay of our family?"

"You're wrong," he argued. "Help has tremendous potential. The partners have invested enough seed money to turn it into a nationwide success. Every time a housewife signs on a new marketer, we reap a profit. We have scores of housewives out conducting parties and recruiting new people every day."

For a time, he was right. Help grew exponentially and made enough of a profit for George to reward his high performers with gold Cadillacs. Of course, the more gold Cadillacs he gave away, the harder the housewives worked.

Everything was going along swimmingly until his affair with Sue blew up in his face. Somehow, her husband caught wind of it and gave her an ultimatum – "either leave the company, or I divorce you and take the children."

Sue quickly caved and her hasty resignation left a gaping hole in the day-to-day operations at Custom Chemicals. I reluctantly cut back on my hours at ADAC and filled in, taking orders and overseeing shipments at the manufacturing plant on Chattahoochee Avenue opposite the Pepsi-Cola bottling plant. Rushing to fill an order before the trucker arrived one day, I was rolling a 55-gallon drum of chemicals to the loading dock when a searing pain ran the length of my spine. I fell to the ground screaming in pain and dear Clyde came running.

"Miz Friedlander, Miz Friedlander are you all right? Should I call an ambulance?"

"I need your help," I said through clenched teeth. "Get someone to take me home."

Despite the agonizing pain from the pulled back muscles and months of physical therapy, I had little choice but to keep a pulse on Custom Chemicals while George kept U.S. Research afloat. When the pain became too intense, I lay down on the hard floor in my office and forwarded Custom Chemical's calls to the house so I could still take orders. Without Clyde's efficiency and ability to take charge at the plant, I could never have done it.

Before long, both businesses unraveled. The California investors had run dry and Help, though profitable for a time, began to fail for lack of money for the day-to-day operations. At Custom Chemicals, sales had been static for months because George had made no effort to reach out for new customers and had ignored the old. As his regulars became dissatisfied with the lackadaisical service, they took their business elsewhere. And there were plenty of eager competitors in Atlanta, a boomtown where industrial chemicals were big business. There's an old Hungarian saying, "You can't be at two weddings with one rear end," and George had defied the odds for too long.

Sue's rapid departure left not only both business, but also George's ego in turmoil. He fell into a major depression so profound that both children expressed concern. Before long, Help Inc. went under and Custom Chemicals was gasping for air.

At the same time, Mother fell and broke her hip and was rushed to Georgia Baptist Hospital by ambulance. The doctor recommended a hip replacement and though we had high hopes for a full recovery, it was not to be. At age ninety, she no longer had the ability to live alone so we had her transferred to Harvest House, a nursing home affiliated with the hospital.

Mother's health deteriorated rapidly; before long, she even refused to eat, which necessitated a feeding tube. To coax her into taking a few bites by mouth, I drove across town each evening in rush hour traffic. At night, I worked on the payable and receivable accounts for Custom Chemicals. To say the least, it was a very trying time.

But some good comes from everything. While Mother was at Harvest House, I became a patient and family advocate and was elected president of the Family Council where I was liaison between Georgia Baptist and the families of patients at Harvest House. I even offered free decorating services while they upgraded the lobby and family meeting areas — activities that gave me leverage to ensure better care for Mother. When she died four years later at the age of ninety-four, it was a tremendous loss. I miss her to this day.

Chapter 20

THE ATLANTA CONSTITUTION, Mon., Oct. 29, 1973 9-1

Man Shot By Bandits Still Serious

By CHUCK BELL

An Atlanta man wounded during a holdup at a drugstore Saturday night remained in serious condition at Piedmont Hospital Sunday while Atlanta police continued searching for the two bandits who shot him and robbed the store of $74 in cash and $100 worth of narcotics.

George Friedlander, , of 875 Wadsworth Drive, was shot once in the forehead when he attempted to flee during the robbery at the Howell Mill Pharmacy, police said.

Homicide Detective Joe Tinsley said Sunday medical reports indicate that Friedlander was shot with a .32 caliber pistol and that fragments of the bullet are still lodged in his head.

The robbery occurred at about 8:40 p.m. Saturday when two white men, both armed with pistols, entered the store and ordered employes Burl Maurer, Barbara Whitaker, Milton Garat and Bill Maurer and Friedlander, to move to the rear of the pharmacy and lie

253

George eventually regained his equilibrium from the loss of Help Inc., and looked toward Canada to breathe new life into Custom Chemicals. One Saturday afternoon while he was catching up on paperwork, two young men from a leading Canadian chemical company called him at the office. He phoned me from there.

"They want to meet with me Monday morning for talks about a joint venture to use my formulations in new Canadian products," he told me excitedly. "Can you make sure I have plenty of clean shirts? I just made a plane reservation, but need some money for the trip. On my way home, I'll stop at Howell Mill Pharmacy and ask Bill Mauer if he'll cash a check for me."

I smiled. Bill, the pharmacist and owner, always complained loudly that customers used his pharmacy as their personal bank, but he never turned any of his regulars down — especially not George who had become a colleague.

"I'll be home in a little while," he told me.

About a half-hour later, the phone rang again. "There's been a holdup at the pharmacy," a young woman told me in a quivering voice. "Your husband has been shot. Please come right over. I'm not sure how badly he's been hurt."

"He's still alive, isn't he?"

"Yes, ma'am, but you'd better hurry."

I grabbed my keys and sped down the few short blocks so quickly I beat the ambulance. Two police cars with their lights flashing were parked out front keeping people away, but through the glass door, I could see a small crowd of people milling about. I tried to remain calm as I approached, but could feel my panic mounting.

"My husband has been shot in there," I told the officer posted outside. "You have to take me to him."

He asked my name, then escorted me inside where several other officers were interviewing Bill and his son while a few dazed customers waited their turn. I hurriedly picked my way through the aisles until I spotted George, paler than the white handkerchief he was pressing against his forehead, propped up against shelves in the center aisle. I knelt down and grabbed his free hand.

"Thank God you're alive! What in the world happened?"

"Those bastards shot me point blank, but I think the bullet just grazed me because there's not much blood," he told me. "You always tell me how hard-headed I am."

Thankful that he was able to make a feeble joke, I studied him closely. Other than the blood stains on his shirt and handkerchief, he seemed stable and even tried to get up.

"No way," I said. "You're not moving until the paramedics check you out."

They arrived moments later and immediately took his vital signs. "Your blood pressure is a little high but otherwise you look fine, Dr. Friedlander," one told him. "The wound is likely superficial, but we need to take you to Piedmont Hospital for x-rays. You're a very lucky man."

As they loaded George onto a gurney and wheeled him to the ambulance, I could see the worried looks on everyone's faces. I dashed out to the car to meet them at the hospital. By the time I had parked, George was in an examination room and the physician sent me out in the waiting area. I was pacing up and down when I spotted our neighbor, Jack Hubert, whose son was a friend of

Lewis's. "I heard on the radio that George had been shot in a hold up," he said. "How is he and what can I do for you, Eva?"

I was in the process of telling him that the bullet had just grazed George when an intern came in and told me that they were cleaning him up and would release him shortly. "I'll let you know when he's ready to go home."

A half-hour later as Jack and I waited, the intern came out again. "I have some bad news," he said. "The bullet is lodged in Dr. Friedlander's forehead and it has to be removed immediately. I'll take you back to see him."

Shortly thereafter, Lynne rushed in. She was home from college and had been babysitting at a neighbor's when the parents came home early. "We heard on the radio that your father was shot in a holdup at Spring Lake Pharmacy," the husband told her. "Grab your things and I'll take you to Piedmont Hospital." Lewis, who had been watching television with friends at his apartment, saw a news bulletin and rushed over, arriving just after his sister.

Before walking into the exam room, Lynne braced for the worst, expecting to find her father unconscious. Instead, he was holding court with Jack and me. George clasped her hand in his and quipped, "I needed this like a hole in the head."

Then he took charge. "No Saturday night intern is going to cut on my brain," he barked. I want you to call Dr. William Moore, Eva. He's the best neurosurgeon in Atlanta and I want him to do the procedure."

There was one major problem, Dr. Moore was in St. Simons on a golfing weekend and it would take five or six hours to drive to Atlanta. "It would be best to have the surgery immediately," he told me. "But if he's willing to wait, I'll start back now."

I put my hand over the phone and told George what Dr. Moore had said and once again urged him not to wait. He was not to be dissuaded. The doctor on duty was so annoyed at George ignoring for his advice, he made him sign a release for ignoring surgery against medical orders.

As we waited through the night, George tried to reconstruct the events at the pharmacy for us. "Bill and I went behind the swinging doors where drugs are stored to talk about a new medication on the market, then came back out front to look through his Physicians Drug Reference," he said. "The pharmacy wasn't crowded, but there were a few other people shopping, including two men who wandered back toward us. When Bill asked, "May I help you?" one of them pulled out a gun and said something to Bill like, 'don't touch the button,' then grabbed him around the neck with one arm and pointed the gun at his head with the other. It all happened so quickly. They yelled at everyone to get down on the floor and not to move. I didn't duck right away because I thought it was a Halloween prank. When I realized the seriousness of the situation, I tried to comply, but I suppose my movement spooked them. The guy holding the gun on Bill dragged him toward me. The next thing I remember hearing is the crack of a gun and then pressure in my head."

The enormity of what had happened hit us all and by morning we were exhausted with worry. Dr. Moore arrived around five in the morning and within a few minutes an orderly came to wheel George off to prep him for the operation. We waited helplessly, fearing that the long wait with a bullet lodged in his skull had done George irreparable harm.

The surgery took an agonizing five hours. Finally, Dr. Moore emerged holding the bullet in his hand. "Dr. Friedlander is one lucky man," he said. "The bullet hit the frontal bone, the thickest part of his forehead, but didn't break through. I think he just used up one of his nine lives."

Though Dr. Moore recommended plastic surgery to repair the deep indentation in George's forehead, he decided against it. "I'm lucky I didn't lose my mental faculties or any more of my vision," he said. "I don't have much sight left and I'm worried that additional surgery would do more harm than good."

Word didn't travel as fast in 1973 as it does today, but by morning, both major newspapers had the story on the front page. Still, we didn't learn all the details until many months later after the two assailants were arrested in Florida trying to rob another pharmacy. They were tried and convicted on multiple counts for a series of holdups and both received life sentences – hardly worth the risk to steal a grand total of seventy-four dollars in cash and one-hundred dollars worth of narcotics from the pharmacy.

Several months after George recovered from the physical and emotional trauma of the holdup, he broached the subject about suing Bill.

"He should have had an adequate alarm system at the pharmacy, which is so ripe for robberies," he told me angrily. "I'm still furious that he was too afraid to activate the existing system and summon the police *before* I was shot. Nothing will make up for the terror I felt after being shot in the head, but winning a law suit would be small satisfaction for the pain I suffered. Besides, I don't want the same thing to happen to anyone else."

"Do you think re-hashing that horrific experience out in court will churn it all up again?" I asked.

"It might, but even so, I want to go ahead."

After several conversations with his attorney, George brought suit against the pharmacy on grounds that the alarm system was inadequate and should have been installed in a way that better protected the customers.

When the case finally came to trial months later, I sat next to George in the courtroom listening in rapt attention. Like other episodes in his life, the transcript of the incident read like a screenplay.

Bill was the primary witness and the following is an account of his testimony taken directly from the transcript. "After the man with the gun shot George, I knew he was going to shoot me too, so I put my hand over my face," Bill said on the stand. "It should be anywhere but my face."

"The man ordered everyone in the store to lie down on the floor and told his partner to stand guard over George. He had a gun too. Both of them were wild-eyed, like they were hyped up on drugs and the man holding the gun on me demanded Dilaudid. I was so terrified I wasn't thinking very clearly, but it occurred to me that since neither George nor I were wearing lab coats, the men likely didn't know which one was the pharmacist.

"I didn't get a good look at the second man," Bill continued, "but I could see that the guy holding the gun on me was getting more agitated. The next thing I remember was him saying, 'How do you open this cash register?' He was still holding me at gunpoint when he reached over the counter, opened the register and snatched up a wad of cash. Then he yelled at his partner, 'Let's get out of here,' and the two of them bolted out the door."

On the stand, Bill admitted he was so traumatized at having a gun to his neck and seeing George get shot, he could barely function — even after the crisis had passed. Fortunately, his son, who also worked in the pharmacy, had the presence of mind to activate the alarm and summon the police.

Despite Bill's admission that he was too frightened to act and all the testimony from the witnesses in the pharmacy at the time of the robbery, the judge ruled that the alarm system was adequate.

George was livid at the outcome. He felt it was another gross injustice in his life — first his interment in three forced labor camps, then the failure of the Italian government to secure his release from Andrassy 60, finally this failed lawsuit. He stormed around for days vowing to take the case to the Georgia Supreme Court if he had to but, on the advice of his attorney, reluctantly decided not to carry the matter forward.

Chapter 21

Life rocked on with little change in the status quo. But despite all the acrimony between us, our joint pride in our children never wavered. George strongly encouraged Lewis to take pre-med courses during his first few years at UGA, but for a time, Lewis toyed with the idea of becoming an architect. I think he made his final decision when his first serious girlfriend convinced him to go into medicine because she was studying to become a nurse.

George was beyond thrilled when our son was accepted at the Medical College of Georgia in Augusta —

one of his own big regrets. Lewis had the aptitude as well as the dedication and was offered an internship at Emory University, followed by residency in emergency room medicine in Miami, where George and I visited frequently. It was a double bonus for George whose ardor for the city had never waned.

Her father's affairs and outbursts had always been an enigma to Lynne, but while taking psychology courses at UGA, she became convinced that George was not only narcissistic but had undiagnosed Type II Bi-polar disorder with depression. "He was so prone to rages that I was afraid to leave you home alone with him when I went off to college," she told me. "He needed a supporting cast, not another star of the show. He clearly saw that as his role and fed himself through relationships outside the marriage. He always blamed someone else when things went badly and you were the closest one around. I can't understand why you stayed with him."

Why, indeed? I questioned my decision frequently, both during his periods of verbal and physical abuse and his multiple affairs. Hardly a day went by that I didn't question the effect that it had on the children.

At the same time, life wasn't all bad. George never apologized, but usually made amends in some other way by bringing home a set of china I had admired, some unusual plants for the garden or expensive gifts from his trips. Despite the inability to stay faithful, he never once made a move to leave me. Perhaps it was our intellectual compatibility. Perhaps it was our shared experiences during the war years. Perhaps he loved me despite his inability to remain faithful. Whatever the reason, I never gave up hope that we would somehow come full circle and rekindle our torrid romance.

Meanwhile, I fortified my own self-esteem by continually improving my knowledge of art, antiques and art history. That was my lifeline and I held on to the things that would help me achieve and overcome rather than collapse and succumb.

When Lynne had her first big love affair, we decided to continue paying the rent on her apartment at UGA even after she moved in with her boyfriend — just in case things didn't work out. It was a good decision. Her so-called "soul mate" had an affair with her former roommate while they were still dating. Lynne was devastated. The failed romance paled in comparison to her emotions when the ex-boyfriend and her ex-roommate were killed in a tragic car accident. George and I were in shock and talked of nothing else for days. What if Lynne had been sitting in the passenger seat? The thought gave us nightmares. It was the second time one of our children had had a close encounter with death in a car.

We were thrilled when following graduation, Lynne was accepted in UGA's highly rated veterinary school, where competition for entrance was even more difficult than medical school. For her, it was the culmination of a dream that had begun years earlier during her "All Creatures Great and Small" and Meathead days.

Once she received her D.V.M., we had three doctors in the family — a source of button-popping pride. I always loved answering the phone when someone asked to talk to "Dr. Friedlander." I could just imagine the look on their faces when I replied, "Which one? Dr. George? Dr. Lewis? or Dr. Lynne?" One day I received a personal bill from Sears addressed to Dr. Eva Friedlander and I joked with the authentic Friedlander doctors that I had graduated from the "University of Sears."

Lewis followed his residency in Miami with another at Yale University Hospital, then, always the homebody, he returned to Atlanta to practice in various emergency rooms in and outside of Atlanta before establishing his own cosmetic surgery practice.

Lynne, on the other hand, was eager to fly the nest and accepted her first job in Newnan, Ga. For a time, she lived her childhood fantasy of a farm girl caring for large animals, but eventually she came to the realization that it was not totally safe for her to traipse out alone in the middle of the night to tend to injured or sick animals.

One day when she was at the house, she dropped a bombshell. "I've found a job with a corporation that manages animal clinics in California," she said. "I'll be moving in the next few weeks."

I peppered her with questions: where would she live? Was she going to drive more than two-thousand miles alone? Was it safe for a pretty young girl to live on her own?

George was more supportive. "Congratulations," he said, giving her a hug. "I think you've made a wise decision."

While Lynne and I chatted about the logistics of packing up her apartment, clothes and pets, George, who was suffering from an extremely painful attack of gout, returned to his easy chair and propped up his foot. I wasn't sure whether his somewhat cavalier reaction was the result of thinking Lynne's decision was sound, or if he was just eager to get off his red, swollen foot.

Once she left, he turned to me. "You're over-reacting," he said. "Lynne is not a child any longer. Remember, you left your mother in Budapest to join me in Rome and then we moved six-thousand miles away across the Atlantic Ocean to America. Your mother survived. You will too."

Still, I fretted day and night. I had become accustomed to Lynne living away from home, but she had always been close enough that I could drive over to see her for the day, or she could come home for the weekend. Was it payback time for leaving my mother in the lurch or just the way life unfolds naturally?

The timing of her departure couldn't have been worse for me. After trying for months to convince George to visit his critically ill sister, Klari, he had left for Budapest just days before.

On the day Lynne came to say goodbye, her face was full of anticipation. I put on a happy face and tried my best to send her off with a smile instead of tears. But what small gesture would show her how much I loved her? Finally, it came to me. While she was in the house picking up a few last minute belongings, I cut one perfect long stemmed red rose from my garden and laid it across the passenger seat.

"Promise you'll call every night to let me know you're okay?" I begged.

Lynne nodded. "I'll be fine, Mom. Please don't worry."

Easy for her to say! I stood in the driveway waving until her car — loaded to the gills with all her belongings, plus the dog and cat — disappeared down the street. Then I turned and dropped down on a chair near the koi pond and sobbed. She was off to California to find a new life. George was abroad, and I was left at home, feeling lonely and a bit sorry for myself.

George remained in Budapest for several months, keeping in touch by phone. His explanation was reasonable enough. "I'm trying to liquidate Klari's apartment so she can move into a smaller place that's easier to keep up after her recovery, but it's taking longer than I expected," he told me repeatedly. I was somewhat suspicious, particularly since he was unusually attentive, rarely failing to tell me how much he missed me or to inquire about Lynne and Lewis.

It wasn't until much, much later when I was putting clean clothes in his top dresser drawer that I ran across a sizeable stack of receipts. The one on the top was from the InterContinental Hotel, Budapest's most beautiful and expensive establishment, the home to visiting dignitaries and royalty. With spectacular views of the Danube, the Royal Palace and the Chain Bridge, the InterContinental was the very spot we always dreamed of staying, but could never justify the cost.

I could feel my anger rising as I flipped through the receipts, all dated during the time George had been visiting Klari. Most were for a couple. A room with a double bed. Two breakfasts at Corso. Two dinners at Gundel, two cognacs and desserts at Café New York. Two tickets to a performance at the Erkel Theater.

I crumbled the stack of bills in my hand and stormed into the kitchen where George was still eating breakfast.

"Didn't you tell me that you stayed in Klari's apartment while you were in Budapest and that she was too ill to join you for dinner until the last week or so?"

"Of course. Why do you ask?"

I raised my clutched fist and tossed the pile of receipts on top of his scrambled eggs. "Because I found these in your top drawer while I was putting your clean laundry away."

"Has your paranoia driven you to snooping into my personal belongings?" he accused.

"I hardly think that's the point. Just who were you sleeping with while Klari was so ill?"

George's face colored slightly and suddenly I understood.

"It was Sadie," I said. "You took her with you."

He blinked, almost imperceptively, but I knew I had nailed him.

"I won't dignify your silly allegation with an answer," he said. With that, he walked out the door, leaving me to seethe once again.

~~~~~~~~

Someone once told me that women who are cheated on either become bitter, or become better. And in many ways, it was true for me. While I swallowed my pride time and again over George's continual obsession with Sadie — and other women — his infidelity forced me to grow as a person and reach a higher level in my professional life than would have been possible had he been faithful. Ironically, those same obsessions likely kept him from achieving *his* potential as a scientist, business man, father and husband.

As for George and me, little changed after the revelation that Sadie had been with him in Budapest. We continued to live in what I called "white zones" that careened from the heat of the Sahara Desert to the deep freeze of Antarctica.

For Lynne, life in California surpassed even her high expectations. She loved her job, being far, far away from the turmoil of life at home, and living near the beach. She also met Marc Goldman, the man who would become her husband two years later.

Their wedding in Yosemite Park amphitheater — the park's first — was straight out of a movie set. The natural rock formation with stone seating resembled a Roman forum and in the distance, we could see Bridal Veil Fall. As the sun set, a kaleidoscope of colors lit up the sky as four men, including Lewis, held the traditional Jewish chuppah or wedding canopy.

Just before George was ready to walk Lynne down the aisle, he turned toward her. I thought he would comment on losing a daughter-gaining a son, Lynne's beauty as a bride or the perfection of the setting. Instead, he preened a little and asked, "How do I look?" It was such a typically George remark that Lynne burst out laughing.

The lovely family affair could have turned out far differently. In fact, George's presence at his daughter's wedding was in question when he experienced shortness of breath just a week before we were to leave for California. The diagnosis was a carotid artery blockage which necessitated immediate surgery. It was performed the very next day and we worried that it would derail his trip to attend his daughter's wedding. I planned to go, with or without him. In the end, he made a supreme effort, a decision he never regretted.

Romance was definitely in the air, at least for my children because shortly after Lynne's wedding, Lewis met Judy, a divorced pet store manager with three children. The two fell in love very quickly and a year later, their first child, Eva Marie, was born, followed five years later by Katarina — close in age to Lynne and Marc's two wonderful children, Jeremy and Ella.

Chapter 22

The years flew by with few highs or lows. I buried myself in my work of doing appraisals and buying and selling antiques, content to build my business. George's interest in Custom Chemicals, on the other hand, waned after the shooting incident. The Canadian company had long since lost interest and, as more competitors appeared on the industrial chemical scene through the years, the company began to flounder. In desperation, he approached our dear friend, Fred Baumgarten, for a loan.

Fred was an extremely successful entrepreneur who had started a small import paper business from his kitchen table and turned it into a hugely profitable endeavor. Through the years, he had been a great resource for George, guiding him around many roadblocks. Most importantly, he had lent George money twenty years prior to travel to Vienna to try and rescue our family members in the aftermath of the Hungarian uprising. He and his wife, Marianne, had also been sympathetic sounding boards for me during my husband's many liaisons.

This time, when George asked for a loan to shore up the business, Fred refused. He felt that George had never put forth the effort to take Custom Chemicals to the next level and make it a huge success. In my mind, Fred was trying to light a fire under George to get the business back on its feet. Regardless the motivation, it backfired. George was so furious that he severed all connections with Fred and Marianne and insisted that I do too. Again, I acquiesced to his wishes, but it was a huge blow to me. They had been our mentors and surrogate American parents and I treasured the friendship.

The incident was a watershed moment for George. He put Custom Chemicals up for sale. After several promising negotiations failed, a family from North Carolina with a successful chemical business purchased it. As part of the contract, George was to remain there for a time during the transition period. I hoped he would stay on even after the initial contract ended, but he made his position quite clear. "I have no interest in being second banana in the business I built with my own hands," he said.

To occupy his time, he resigned from the Democratic Party after Ronald Reagan's election and crossed over to the Republican camp with a vengeance. He volunteered on committees, contributed financially, and received numerous certificates for his service. I suppose he was satisfying his unfulfilled desire to enter the political arena. His retirement also allowed him to participate more fully in the Regional Foreign Policy Conferences sponsored by the Department of State; he traveled frequently abroad as part of this prestigious group.

By that time, I had joined four experienced antique dealers in a lovely co-op we named Antiques of Vinings. Except for a one-day-a-week obligation, I had the freedom to come and go as I pleased and to continue working in the business I loved. George was pleased with the posh surroundings of the shop and dropped in to compliment us on the high quality antiques we carried. On occasions like my birthday or our anniversary, he always sent massive bouquets. My partners oohed and aahed over his romantic gestures, but I always felt it was more of a show to appear as an ideal husband rather than out of real affection for me.

Shortly after I joined the group, a friend introduced me to Betty Woodruff, the daughter of deceased Atlanta artist, Ben Shute. She knew Betty was looking for someone to represent the esteemed painter who had initially come to Atlanta on a temporary teaching assignment at the newly established High Museum School of Art. He ended up staying for the remainder of his life and led the fine arts, commercial art and advertising school into a dynamic institution which later became the Atlanta College of Art.

What an honor! Not only was he a co-founder of the art school, Shute had made a name for himself with portraiture. But I always felt his true strength was in the hundreds of paintings documenting his travels. No matter where he went, whether St. Simons, Ga., Italy, Portugal or Maine, he came home with dozens of watercolors that captured the essence of place. Shute won scores of prestigious awards and his work was exhibited at the Museum of Modern Art in New York, the Art Institute in

Chicago, the Corcoran Gallery of Art in Washington. I was truly honored to sell his paintings at Vinings Antiques and to represent Shute's second wife, Keenan, a gifted artist in her own right. Even George was impressed. Happily, our successful collaboration continues in my space at the Historic Roswell Antique Market.

Another pleasant surprise was a letter from Steven Spielberg's Survivors of the Shoah Visual History Foundation in Los Angeles asking that we tell our stories for the project that records video testimony from survivors of the Holocaust. I was eager to participate, but George refused. "I don't want to tell them my story. They'll steal it and use it for a movie plot," he said.

I just laughed. His response was so typical of his mistrust of everyone but himself. It was also comical. "If they want to make a movie out of my story, it's fine with me," I said. "I'm sure Steven Spielberg would pay handsomely for the rights."

A few weeks later, representatives from the Shoah Foundation came to the house where I did a two-hour video interview and posed for pictures. In a rare change of heart, George decided to pose for the picture and Lewis arrived at the house just in time to join us. The year after George died, I was asked to do another interview with the William Breman Jewish Heritage and Holocaust Museum. I consider it a great honor to have been selected for both. Hopefully young people will learn from these testimonies so the Holocaust will never be repeated.

As George neared eighty, his eyesight deteriorated drastically and he had little or no sight in one eye due to glaucoma and very little in the other. Yet he continued to dress each morning in a smart business suit and one of his seventy-five blue shirts, then spent twenty minutes agonizing over the selection of one of his one-hundred imported silk ties. "You act like you're going to meet with Ronald Reagan himself," I chided. One day he asked me to drive him to Rich's to buy a new pair of shoes. I was amused that even then, he was so vain that he explained to the salesman that he was wearing orthopedic shoes because was recovering from a "sports injury."

On most mornings, his retirement routine was the same. He primped, then picked up his briefcase loaded with crossword puzzles, walked out the door, and climbed into the car. When I questioned the advisability of driving, considering his eyesight, he generally said he was going to the Northside library. "Whenever I plan going farther or to the downtown library, I call Jonah at Yellow Cabs. Today, my eyes are pretty clear and I may stop at Rich's to buy a new tie." I chuckled to myself about his habit of making a purchase one day, then going back to return it the next. In truth, I was relieved that he found something to occupy his time while I was at the shop.

Just minutes after George drove off one morning, I left for work but decided to stop at the grocery store. I wanted to pick up some fruit for lunch so I wouldn't have to leave my partner alone during the noon hour. I was getting into the car when I noticed George's Cadillac in the parking lot on the lower level. He rarely went to that shopping area and I became concerned that he had experienced heart palpitations and had stopped to place a nitroglycerin tablet under his tongue. If that was the case, he certainly shouldn't be driving and I could take him back home.

I dropped the groceries in the trunk and was walking toward his car when I saw a blue Lincoln Town Car pull up next to his. It looked vaguely familiar. Then the door opened and Sadie stepped out. Undoubtedly, I had discovered their meeting place.

I fumed all day to my business partner and was so furious that I confronted him the moment I walked in the door. "I saw you get into Sadie's car this morning. You're at it again, aren't you?"

"You're mistaken," he lied. "I was at the library all day doing research."

"Research? Research on what? My eyesight is far from perfect but there was no mistaking Sadie. She's still driving a blue Lincoln Town Car.

He went on the defensive. "I didn't tell you because I knew your reaction would be just like this," he said. "She just lost her husband and needs her old friends. There's nothing between us. I just feel sorry for her. Besides, I wanted to go to the downtown library and she knows my eyesight is too poor to drive in all that traffic. When she offered me a lift, I accepted."

Without another word, I turned on my heel and stormed out the door. I had no idea where I was going. I just knew I didn't want to be anywhere near George.

~~~~

True to form, George refused to admit that he and Sadie had rekindled the flickering flame. "You're paranoid," he said. "I'm an old man. She's an old woman. You give me far more credit as a Don Juan than I deserve."

On the one in a million chance that she was just acting as his chauffeur, I waited for an hour after he left the next morning, then called Jonah. "Why don't you take me where you frequently take my husband," I told him.

"Ma'am, you want to go over to that big house on West Paces Ferry?" he asked. My heart sank. West Paces was Sadie's street.

"Yes, please, Jonah."

We drove into the heart of Buckhead through some of Atlanta's most upscale northside neighborhoods past the exclusive Cherokee Town and Country Club and the gracious Greek Revival Governor's Mansion with its thirty columns and well-manicured grounds. I stared vacantly out the window. What did I hope to accomplish with this wild idea?

Jonah slowed down and signaled to turn left into a driveway of a handsome Tudor home partially hidden behind an iron gate. Sadie's house.

"No, no," I said coming to my senses. "Go to the corner, then turn around and pass by the house again very slowly." He glanced over his shoulder and I read his look. He thought I had taken leave of my senses.

"Yes, ma'am," Jonah said.

On our second pass, I strained to get a better look. Sure enough, Sadie's blue Town Car was parked in the circular driveway.

"Should I take you up to the door, Miz Friedlander?"

"Certainly not," I snapped. "Take me home."

I slunk down in the seat, feeling like a foolish old woman. What in the world had I been thinking? I certainly would never admit to George that I had stalked him like a lovesick teenager. What's more, I had embarrassed myself mightily in front of Jonah. Should I ask him not to mention my joy ride to George or just leave it to his discretion?

In order to avoid running into Jonah when he picked George up for what I strongly expected were téte-a-tétes with Sadie, I headed to Vinings Antiques earlier than usual each morning and stayed later at night. I was numb, worn out with the constant arguing and the realization that Sadie had once again inserted herself in our marriage. And George had welcomed her in.

I seesawed back and forth. The same tired thoughts about leaving George ran through my mind. By then, I was also in my mid-eighties with failing eyesight. What would I do? Where would I go? What would my grown children and grandchildren think? I was bone weary with George's ongoing affair with Sadie. Had it continued all during the years she was married? It was so ironic I had to smile. How would she feel if she knew that in addition to being a married man, he had been unfaithful to her with Marjorie and Sue?

The last spark of hope for a turnaround I had kept alive through the years was extinguished. "If I were younger, I would tell you that you have just used up your ninth life, George," I muttered to myself. "But I'm too old and too weary of it all to care."

Chapter 23

Our lives changed drastically in 2002 when Jonah pulled into the driveway to pick George up and found him lying on the ground bleeding profusely from his head. He was obviously in severe pain but fully conscious. "Jonah, thank God you're here. Go into the house and call my son, Lewis," he ordered. "His number is next to the phone in the kitchen."

"Mr. Friedlander, I know your son is a doctor, but we need to call 911. You need help real quick," Jonah insisted.

George was vehement. "No ambulance. Call Lewis. Call my son."

As luck would have it, Lewis was out of the office. Still, George refused to allow Jonah to call 911. "Tell his nurse, Melinda, to come right over."

Melinda arrived in record time and somehow, she and Jonah got George into her car for the short ride to Piedmont Hospital's emergency room. She called me at work from there. "Hurry over to Piedmont, Eva," she said. "George fell head first on the big rock near your driveway and severely injured his right eye."

The prognosis was grim. Due to glaucoma, George had already lost all vision in his left eye and depended on the right to see. Would he lose it too? There was not much the ophthalmologist could do except bandage the eye and hope that some sight would return. We held out high hopes and consulted with numerous specialists. When none could find a solution, we got a referral to the Mayo Clinic in Jacksonville to get another opinion. The diagnosis was the same.

George remained remarkably optimistic. "I think I can see a little more today," he would tell me. "Go out of the room and put on a brightly colored sweater. I want to see if I can guess what color it is." Occasionally, he answered correctly and he was momentarily buoyed. Mostly, it was just pure luck.

Over the next year, his health went from bad to worse. The fall was followed by two heart attacks, the result of a severe kidney problem, and several small strokes. Nitroglycerin helped for a time, but we made so many trips to the emergency room, the intake workers recognized us on sight. Finally, doctors put stents in his heart and kidneys.

As his physical condition weakened, he began having pervasive nightmares about the war years, compounded by daytime hallucinations. He insisted on having sturdy shoes either on or nearby — day and night — so he could "escape" at a moment's notice as he had done during his internment in forced labor camps.

His screams frequently rang out during the night, awakening me from a deep sleep. "Don't you see those dogs? Can't you see the Germans bringing them in? Run, run for your life!" he shouted. After these episodes, he broke out in a cold sweat and shivered so violently that I was afraid he would have another heart attack or fall out of bed and further injure himself. It got to the point that he dreaded the nightmares so much that he was afraid of falling asleep.

On one of his tormented nights, my fears were realized. He woke up around three in the morning and insisted on walking around and around the house on his walker with me at his side. Somehow, the leg of the walker got tangled up in an Oriental rug and he fell like a stone. I had to call the fire department to help me get him back in bed.

My own health took a beating, along with my eyesight, the result of macular degeneration. The problem had escalated to the point that I could scarcely read the dosage on any of our multiple prescription bottles. My blood pressure shot sky high and after one too many scary episodes, my cardiologist insisted that I hire a night nurse so I could get some much-needed rest. George's care during the day remained my total responsibility.

A defining moment came one night when the nurse was off. I was helping George manipulate his walker sideways through the narrow bathroom door – the only way it would fit. When I tried to turn him around, I lost my balance and hit my head against the wall. Fortunately, the fall only resulted in a lump on my head, but it scared the wits out of me. What if I had been knocked unconscious? George would be unable to find the phone to call for help.

The next day, Lewis called a family conference and the four of us decided that the best course of action was for George to enter Nursecare, a highly rated nursing home, "temporarily." Everyone but George knew that the move was permanent, but we let him hope.

At first, it seemed a decent solution. Lynne and her family were living in Atlanta temporarily while her husband interviewed for jobs, so she and her children, Jeremy and Ella, were able to visit George frequently. He loved listening to cartoons with Jeremy and having little Ella crawl all over the bed. "Do you know that you were named for Ella Fitzgerald, one of my favorite jazz singers?" he asked her. She giggled, having no notion what he was saying, but delighted to be the center of attention.

With the assistance of private nurses, George's overall health improved. He even seemed relatively content. He also relished the times when Lewis brought his daughter, Eva Marie, to visit. At age four, she was too big to crawl on the bed, but the two of them would have long conversations about whatever popped into Eva Marie's head.

To while away the hours, he listened to the radio, usually tuned in to his beloved jazz or international soccer games. He never tired of hearing repeats of movies and television shows featuring The Three Stooges, Groucho Marx or James Bond. He and Lewis had seen re-runs of The Stooges so many times over the years that they could recite Mo, Larry, and Curly's dialogue in sync with the movie or television show, then laugh hilariously. As for James Bond, George always fancied himself the prototype for the famous spy and reveled in every reel, often pointing out similarities between his own daring escapades during the war years and Agent 007's.

A year after he entered Nursecare, I had a hip replacement and recuperated just two floors away from George. As my mobility improved, I spent most of the day in his room where we had our meals and talked. Those weeks gave me insight into his everyday routine and I became more sympathetic to the monotony of long days of ill health with few diversions.

As unhappy and bitter as I had been over George's long-standing relationship with Sadie, my animosity gradually evaporated during the two years I cared for him. That euphoric, heady romantic love that had consumed me in post-war Hungary and Italy was long gone, but so was the loathing I felt during his multiple affairs. Strangely, I felt compassion for the man I had lived with for fifty-five years of my life.

During the long days in the nursing home when I kept him company, we reminisced about the ups and downs of raising children. Reels of film turned in our minds. Vacations in Miami, Jamaica and Ibiza. President Johnson's inauguration. Lynne and Lewis's doctorates. Swearing our allegiance to America, winning the DAR award. George's coup in getting Atlanta's first professional soccer team, the Atlanta Chiefs, to the city. His participation in foreign trade associations. My art lecturing and certification as an antique appraiser, the years at Rich's. Owning my own business — all the happy things that had been overshadowed by our marital troubles.

The only major argument we had during those last two years came when our friend, Hugh Cates, learned that

George had never written a will. I was dumbfounded. My husband had long since used up his nine lives. Didn't he realize that his luck was about to run out? How could a man who maintained for more than 50 years that *he* had the only head for business in the family failed to take care of this vital piece of business?

I insisted that he rectify it immediately. He balked. Finally, Hugh persuaded him that a will was vital to protect his assets for the children and me. Within the week, our attorney came by the nursing home to draw it up. It was a great relief to have that important document in hand, particularly at a time when his health was so precarious.

We carefully avoided any discussion of Sadie and, as far as I was concerned, she had disappeared from our lives forever — until Lewis called me at home one evening. "Mom, I got a call from Sadie today," he said. "Dad must have told her he was in a nursing home and she's been secretly visiting him for the past few months. She wants to come more regularly and, in exchange, she is offering to help defray the expenses of his private duty nurses."

"Who does she think she is visiting my husband behind my back?" I yelled. "Some nerve she has. No. No. I forbid her from going to the nursing home even one more time. I don't want a dime from that woman. I don't care how badly I need the money."

And need it, I did. Although Medicare and our supplemental insurance paid the bulk of his medical expenses, we had to pay the nursing home plus private nurses to the tune of two-thousand dollars per month ourselves. It was eating through our savings faster than boll weevils devoured the South's cotton crops. Every time I paid his bills and our household expenses, I worried about how long our savings would last and how I could supplement my personal income if something happened to him.

Lewis brought up Sadie's proposition repeatedly. "This subject is closed," I told him. Weeks later, Lewis called Lynne in California, and the two of them and their spouses put the pressure on.

"Mom," Lynne insisted, "Sadie has caused you and our family so much grief over the last forty-five years. "Chances are, she still visits Dad, despite your orders to the contrary. It's pay back time. Take her money. You've earned it."

The children also talked to George, who was not the least apologetic about a devotion so deep that Sadie would offer to help him monetarily. "Of course, we should accept her money," he shrugged. "Let her pay. We introduced her to Ben and apparently he left her more money than she will ever need. Why not let her share it with us."

I continued to vacillate for weeks and even shared my dilemma with good friends, who to my surprise agreed with Lynne and Lewis. "But if I accept her offer, I'll be condoning their affair retroactively," I lamented. "The very idea is heinous to me."

They felt just the opposite. "Don't be foolish, Eva. You're not blessing anything. You're getting even."

After considerably more wrangling between pride and practicality, I reluctantly accepted Sadie's offer — on three conditions. She was never to have any direct contact with me. No money was to pass from her hand to mine. Instead, she would take cash to Melinda, Lewis's office manager, who would give it to me to pay the nurses. She could visit only twice a week on Tuesdays and Thursdays — no exceptions.

In fact, Sadie agreed so rapidly I didn't have time to reconsider and, for the most part, she stuck to her word. She rarely came to see George empty handed and even hired a massage therapist to visit several times a week. Sometimes, he enjoyed it, other times he couldn't be bothered and sent the masseuse away. His favorite nurse, Gina, complained that Sadie acted as if she were his wife. "She even insisted that we leave the room so she and Dr. Friedlander could visit in private," Gina told me. "I'm surprised she didn't tell his roommate to get out of his bed."

Sadie and I managed to stay far away from one another for over a year — until I dropped in to visit George on *her* day of the week, planning to leave before her customary mid-afternoon arrival. That morning, I made my usual stop at the snack machine in the lobby to smuggle in some salty treats he loved, then boarded the elevator to his third floor room.

As I passed the nurses' station, the head nurse looked up from her paper work. "Doc's had a good morning but he's restless," she said. "Even Gina can't settle him down. He's been asking for you."

I knew that when Gina couldn't pacify him I had better come up with some amusing conversation. It was easier said than done. Even though he had been at Nursecare for nearly two years, I still found it difficult to see this once dashing man virtually helpless. Throughout our life together, he had surrounded himself with fine period furniture, original art work and tasteful accessories. Now, his only furnishings were that damn recliner Sadie had given him, plus a tiny nightstand from home that concealed his trademark bottle of Giorgio Armani cologne, clandestine snacks, a hairbrush and a small radio he kept tuned to his favorite jazz station. Instead of living with family members, his roommate was a noisy, erratic stranger whose domain was separated only by a cloth curtain.

"It's Eva," I announced, opening the door.

"You're late," George chided. Then that old mischievous grin that mesmerized me as a young woman spread over his face. "It's wonderful that you're here," he said, pointing to the chair next to him. "Did you bring me anything?"

"Guess," I said, playing our silly game.

"Chips? Fritos? Cheetos?" His voice rose hopefully.

"Your favorite," I replied, handing him a bag of Cheetos.

He grinned widely. Despite his blindness, he had no difficulty tearing open the bag of contraband his doctor frowned on. But why deprive him now? These small treats gave him his only diversion in an otherwise hopeless life.

I watched as George lustily savored every bite. With a final flourish, he licked his forefinger and thrust it deep into the bag to make sure he hadn't missed a single crumb. It reminded me of the way we threw good manners to the wind and slid our fingers across plates of Fettuccine Alfredo to scrape off the last bit of rich sauce during our years in Rome.

Another enduring habit was his self-absorption about his appearance. As a sexy, self-assured young man, he had combed his wavy brown hair into an airy pompadour and insisted on wearing clean starched blue shirts that matched his eyes, well-styled suits and Italian silk ties –

even in Budapest following World War II, when most Hungarians felt lucky to have clothes on their backs. Once our finances improved, he had shopped at only the best haberdasheries that sold name brands like his favorite designer, Armani. For him, the act of getting dressed every morning was a stage production.

While other patients lounged around in rumpled pajamas and robes, George's vanity remained intact. He was known to all the staff as "Doc, the patient in room thirty-two who always wears starched blue shirts." Gina and I had laughed at the absurdity and had managed to talk him into wearing soft warm-up pants instead of slacks, but we had given up on talking him out of the shirts. Once or twice when he was feeling particularly poorly, we had tried to sneak on a pajama top, but there was no way to fool him. His slim fingers would glide over the texture of the fabric and he chastised us angrily.

I was relieved that this vain man couldn't still see his reflection in the mirror. His skin was the color of stale white bread and his once chestnut brown hair was white and thinning with an almost comical fringe of brown hair around the collar line, remnants of years of dyeing it. George still wanted Gina to keep up his Lady Clairol routine, but she and I conspired to let his hair whiten naturally. Since days and nights blended into one another at the nursing home, it wasn't hard to convince him that it still looked presentable.

That particular day had gone better than most. George was in a fine mood. We held hands while he gently stroked the soft cashmere of my sweater sleeve. "I think I can see the color you're wearing," he said. "It's brown, isn't it?"

286

Actually, the sweater was aquamarine, but to humor him, I lied. The delighted look on his face convinced me I had done the right thing. How could I help but admire his incredible tenacity to cling to the slim hope that his sight would be restored? I wanted to keep the mood light and chatted about Jeremy, Eva Marie, and Ella's latest escapades and deliberately stayed away from local politics, a subject that sent him into an angry diatribe — unless it pertained to his beloved Republican Party. His main interest was hearing what was happening on the international scene so he could play armchair diplomat and rant that he was far more capable than the current administration. "They should have offered me a Cabinet post," he fumed repeatedly. "They don't know anything."

I had just walked over to drop the empty Cheeto bag into the trashcan when without warning, George became agitated. "Where are my shoes? Are they next to my bed? Hand them to me." He stretched out his hands imploringly.

Once the shoes were safely within his reach, I distracted him by talking about the happy years we spent in Italy after the war when he worked side by side with Dr. Chain on a delivery method for penicillin. "It was the most important work I ever did," he said frequently. "If only our American visas had been deferred for longer, I could have found a faster and better method than the rest of the team." He smiled and squeezed my hand. "When I'm well, let's return to Italy. We were so happy there."

I fell right in step. "Do you remember the time we took off our shoes and waded in the Trevi Fountain until the *polizia* chased us off? How about our "alarm clock," — the newspaper boy yelling, '*Edizione speciale* (extra, extra)!' on the corner as he tried to drum up sales?"

287

For the next few hours, I humored George about returning to Rome together. We talked about where we would stay and even argued about where we would eat our first meal. Ludicrous as it seemed, it was fun to dream again, even make plans despite our combined disabilities. George's health was so precarious he was unable to even come home for a visit and I struggled to keep the household on an even financial keel while dealing with my failing sight.

We were having so much fun reminiscing that I forgot to check the time. When I finally glanced at my watch, I knew I needed to leave immediately or risk running into Sadie. I kissed George on the forehead and stroked his hair.

"Stay a little longer," he begged, clutching my hand. "Please."

"I can't," I said. "Your *other* regular visitor is coming soon. I'll see you tomorrow." I stood and took a few steps away from his bed. At that moment, the door flew open and *she* stood in the door, as surprised to see me as I was to see her.

As I searched for words, George sensed a change in the atmosphere. "Eva, what is it? Are you still here?"

"I'm here, I replied. So is your *other* visitor."

She stammered, "Oh, I'm sorry. I must be early. I'll come back later."

George turned his head in the direction of our voices and his face lit up. He flashed a grin. "Stay," he said. "Both of you. Please."

The old flight or fight syndrome kicked in, but while I was trying to decide, Sadie took my lack of response for a "yes" and slowly walked across the room toward

George's bed. "Guess what I brought you," she cooed, her voice dripping honey.

He sniffed the air. "Fried chicken?" he asked. She giggled and extracted a box of Mrs. Winner's finest from the depths of her shopping bag. The scent of George's spiking cholesterol wafted across the room. I could feel my face flush. Still, I didn't move.

She bent over him and placed a chicken leg tenderly into his mouth, much as one would feed a toddler. I watched George eagerly take a bite or two. Then, he patted the bed on both sides. "Come sit beside me, please," he implored, turning his head, first in my direction, then in hers.

Sadie made small talk as she dragged a chair up to the bed and plopped down. I took a few steps toward the door, undecided about whether to stay and watch them interact — something I had not done in decades — or cling to what was left of my pride and exit.

I chose the latter. I walked back to his bed and kissed him good-by. "I'll be back tonight with Lewis," I told him.

~~~~~

That evening when we returned to visit while George ate dinner, Sadie was long gone. I decided it was best for my blood pressure just to ignore the awkward meeting earlier that day. "I'm not hungry after all that Mrs. Winner's chicken, so let's get right to the entertainment," he said, flashing me a conspiratorial smile.

"I've brought you a Groucho Marx video and a couple of episodes of The Stooges," Lewis said. "Which do you prefer?"

"Need you ask?" he said.

Lewis and Gina helped him move to the recliner so we could all watch *The Three Stooges* on the VCR for the umpteeth time. It was after nine-o'clock when we got up to leave. "Do you have to go now?" George asked. "I'm just getting warmed up."

"Mom is exhausted and I need to take her home then try to get home in time to kiss Eva Marie goodnight. Can I help you get back in bed?"

"Do I have a choice?" George asked.

A few hours later, Lewis received a call from the registered nurse on duty saying that George was restless. "Why don't you wheel him down to the nurse's station for juice and cookies?" he suggested. After two subsequent calls, he told her to give him some Benadryl to help him relax.

My phone rang at four in the morning, startling me from a dead sleep. Lewis was on the line. "Mother, Nursecare just called. Dad died in his sleep. Do you think we should go over and say a final good-bye?"

I was oddly calm. "No, let's remember him as he was tonight watching his favorite Stooges movies and joking with us."

I put down the phone, void of tears. "Ah, George," I whispered. "Our curious journey has ended."

The next few days were a blur of calling friends, planning for his funeral and moving his personal belongings back to the house – except for the recliner Sadie had given him. There was no way it was coming back into my home.

His absence left a huge void in my life. Though I had become accustomed to living alone, I had seen him almost daily and always knew he was *there*. Suddenly, I was truly alone. I felt some satisfaction that during the last two years of his life, we had been able to patch up our damaged relationship and move beyond hatred to come full circle. Despite Sadie's presence, I had few regrets.

Breaking Jewish tradition to bury the dead as soon as possible, we delayed the funeral until Lynne and her family could come from California. During the graveside service at Crestlawn Cemetery, I was gratified to see that so many people from the five decades of our lives in Atlanta had come to pay their respects. My colleagues from Rich's and ADAC, my partners at Vinings Antiques, George's business associates, our long-time accountant, doctors, friends, neighbors, Lewis and Lynne's childhood chums, dear Clyde — all were in attendance.

I sat in the first row under the funeral canopy between Lewis and Lynne and their families and tried to focus on the rabbi's service and the eloquent words of my children. When the rabbi recited the Mourner's Kaddish, an important Jewish ritual in all burials or remembrances, I rose to shovel dirt on George's grave. I was shaking so violently that Lynne had to help support me.

For a few moments, Lynne and I stood silently over the gravesite, each lost in thought. The fifty-five years of our marriage, both good and bad, flashed through my mind. I picked up the heavy shovel, scooped up a pile of Georgia red clay and threw it on top of his coffin. When I heard the loud ka-thunk as it hit, I began to sob. Lynne gently took the shovel from my hands and took her turn. Then, putting a firm hand on my elbow, she led me back to my chair so Lewis and others could follow suit.

As we turned, I heard an audible sob coming from the row behind mine and looked straight at Sadie. She was standing in my shadow much as she had for the last 45 years of our lives. We nodded, acknowledging one another's presence and she whispered her condolences. But by that time, I was surrounded by family and friends. When I looked up again, I caught a glimpse of her walking slowly back to her car. Alone. From out of the blue came something George had said to me on the last day of his life.

"Eva, you are the only woman I ever truly loved."

I want to believe he was speaking his heart.

~~~~~~~~~~~~~~~~~~

www.ninelivesofamarriage.com

Epilogue

Since the first edition of my book, readers have suggested that I bring the book up to date. Many have asked why I continued to stay in a marriage with seemingly insurmountable challenges.

There is no simple answer for such complex issues. I suppose I was desperately trying to rekindle the original fire in our relationship and never really gave up hope that the marriage could be restored. At the very core, despite the difficulties, I remained in love with my husband.

At 90, I'm fiercely independent and try to stay in tune with the rapidly changing world of technology, politics, music, art and theater. My antique business at the Historic Roswell Antique Market continues to bring me interesting challenges in the decorative arts field.

Besides my independent life style, my greatest source of satisfaction comes from watching my children and grandchildren as they blossom.

Miraculously, life goes on.
Eva Friedlander